Love Is In The Air

by
Rolling Voice

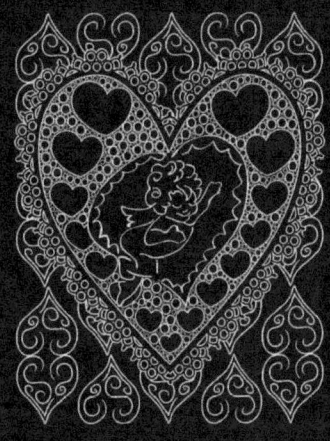

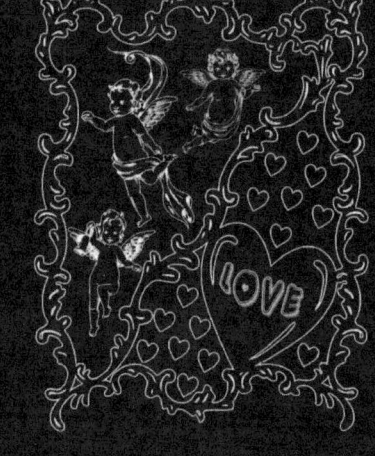

Previews

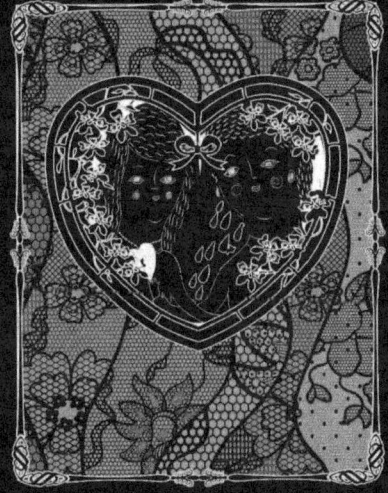
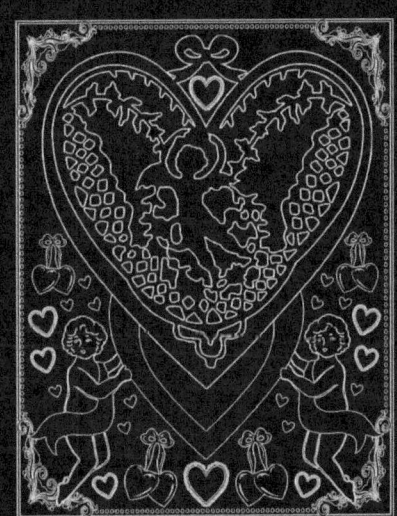
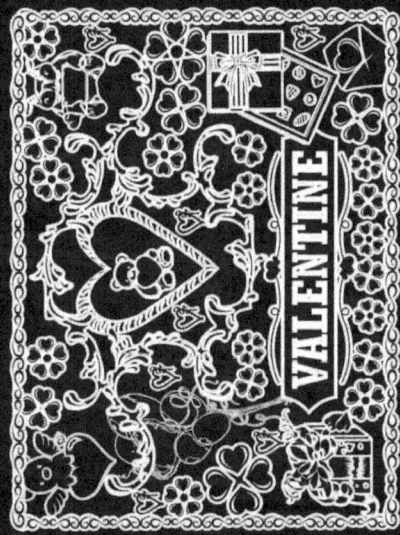

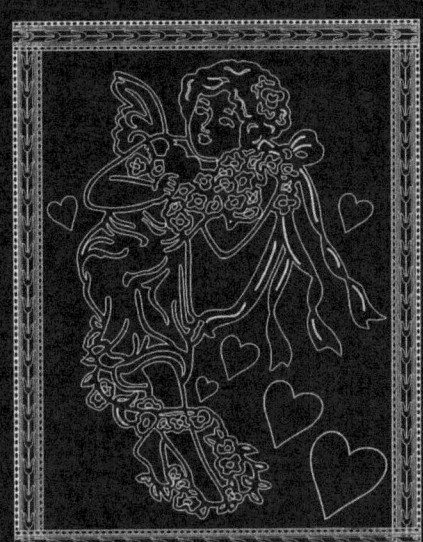

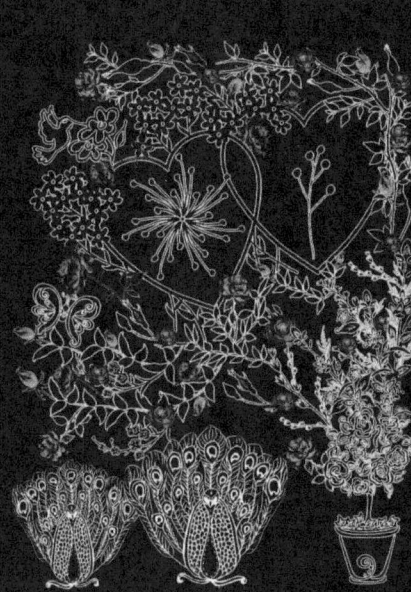

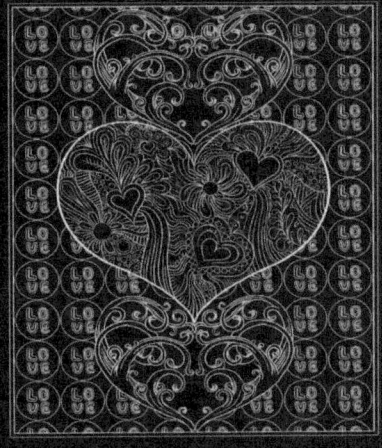
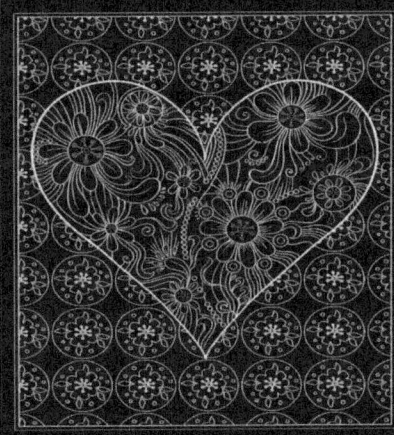
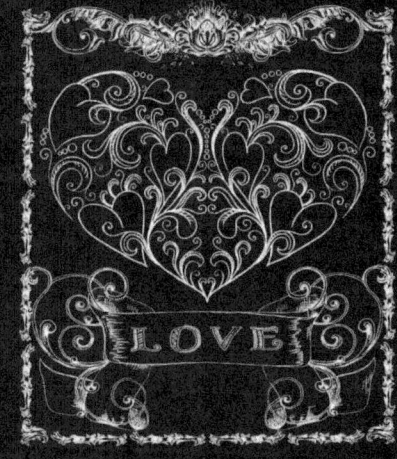

Previews

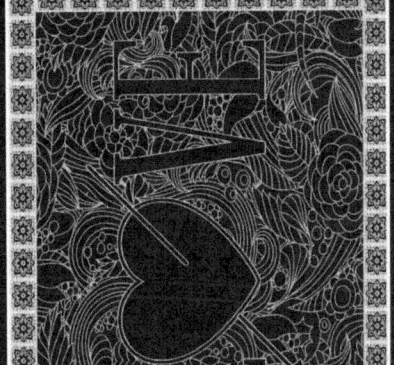
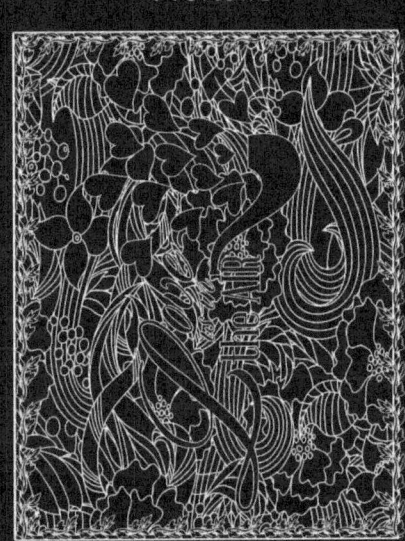
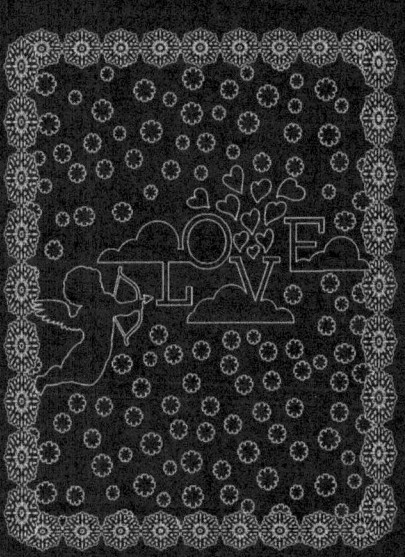

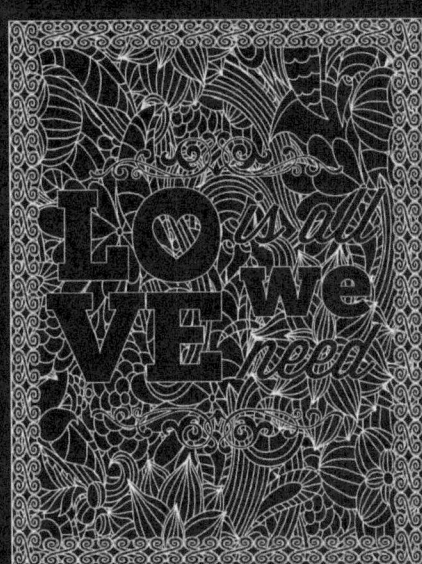
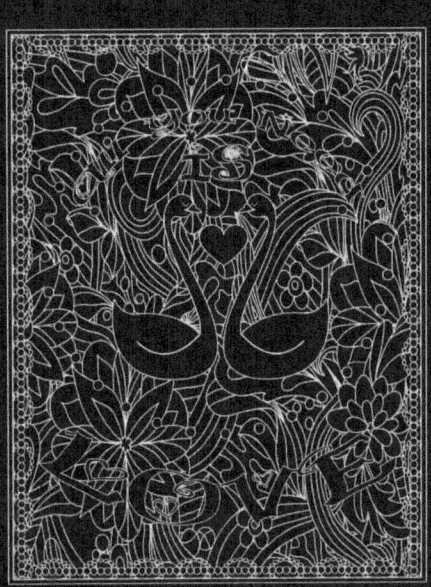
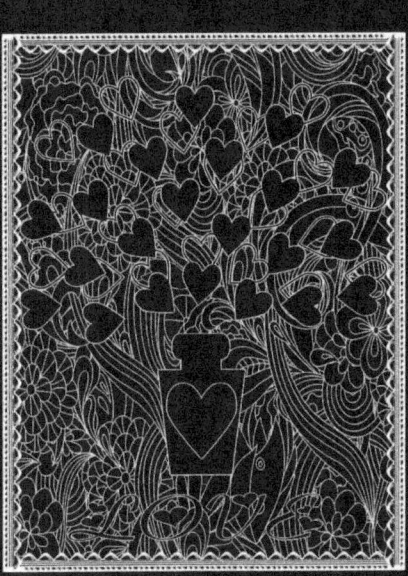

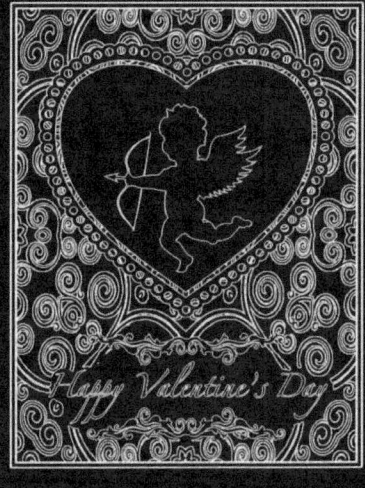
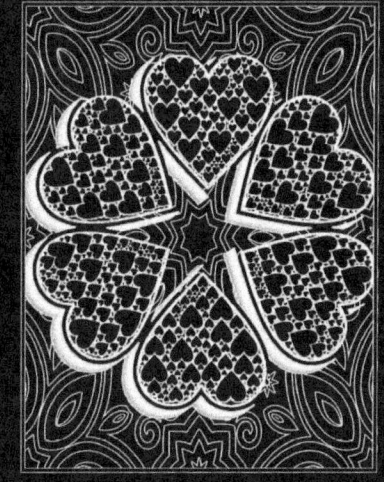
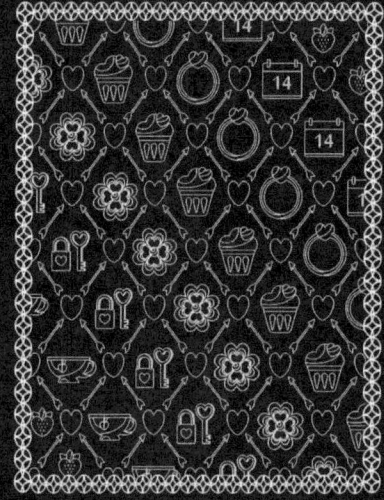

Previews

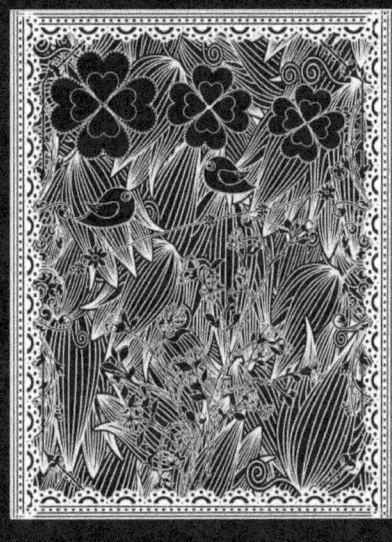

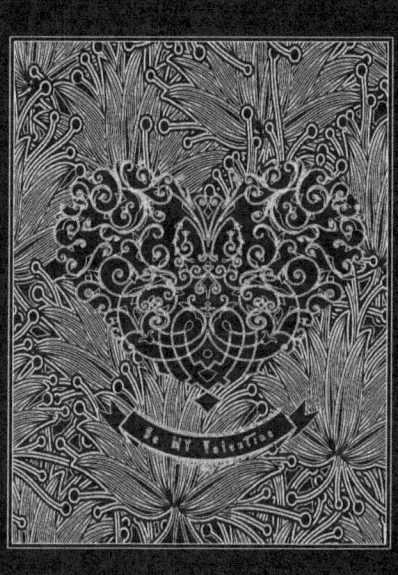

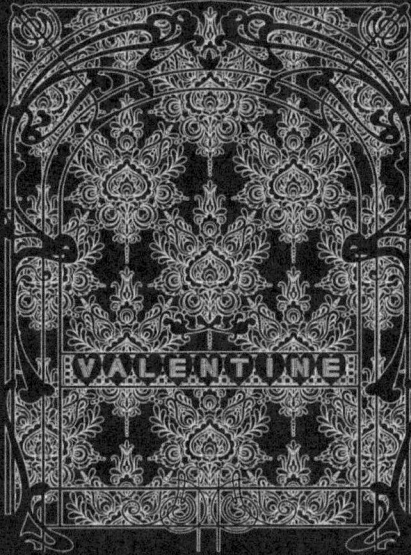
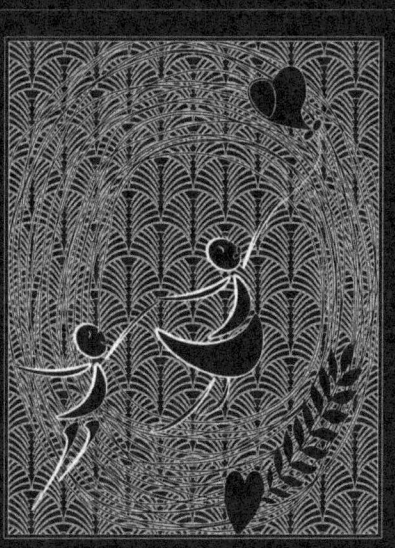
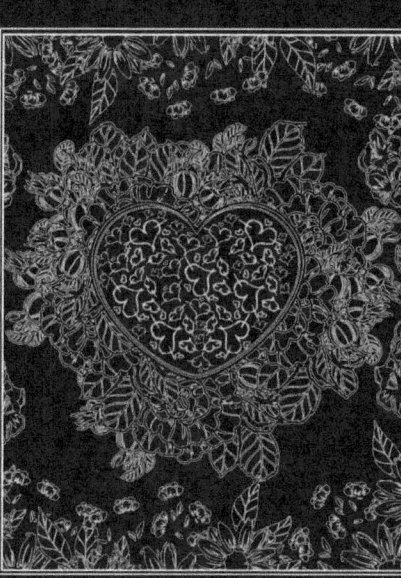

Printed in the United States of America

First Printing, 2016

ISBN-13 : 978-1523898558
ISBN-10 : 1523898550

Rolling Voice Publishing
33 Lower Park, Chartfield Avenue
London, SW15 6QY
United Kingdom

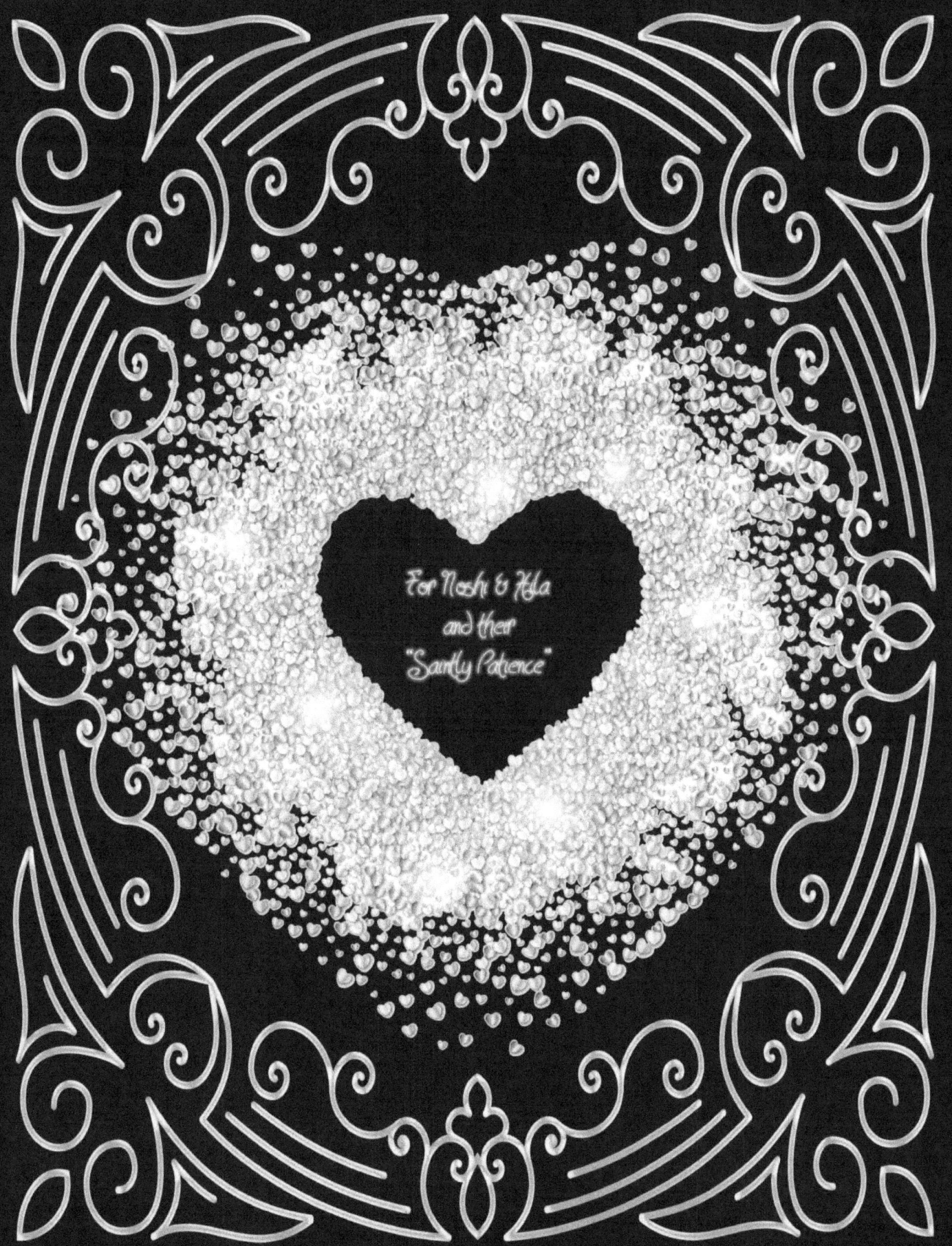

For Noshi & Ayla
and their
"Saintly Patience"

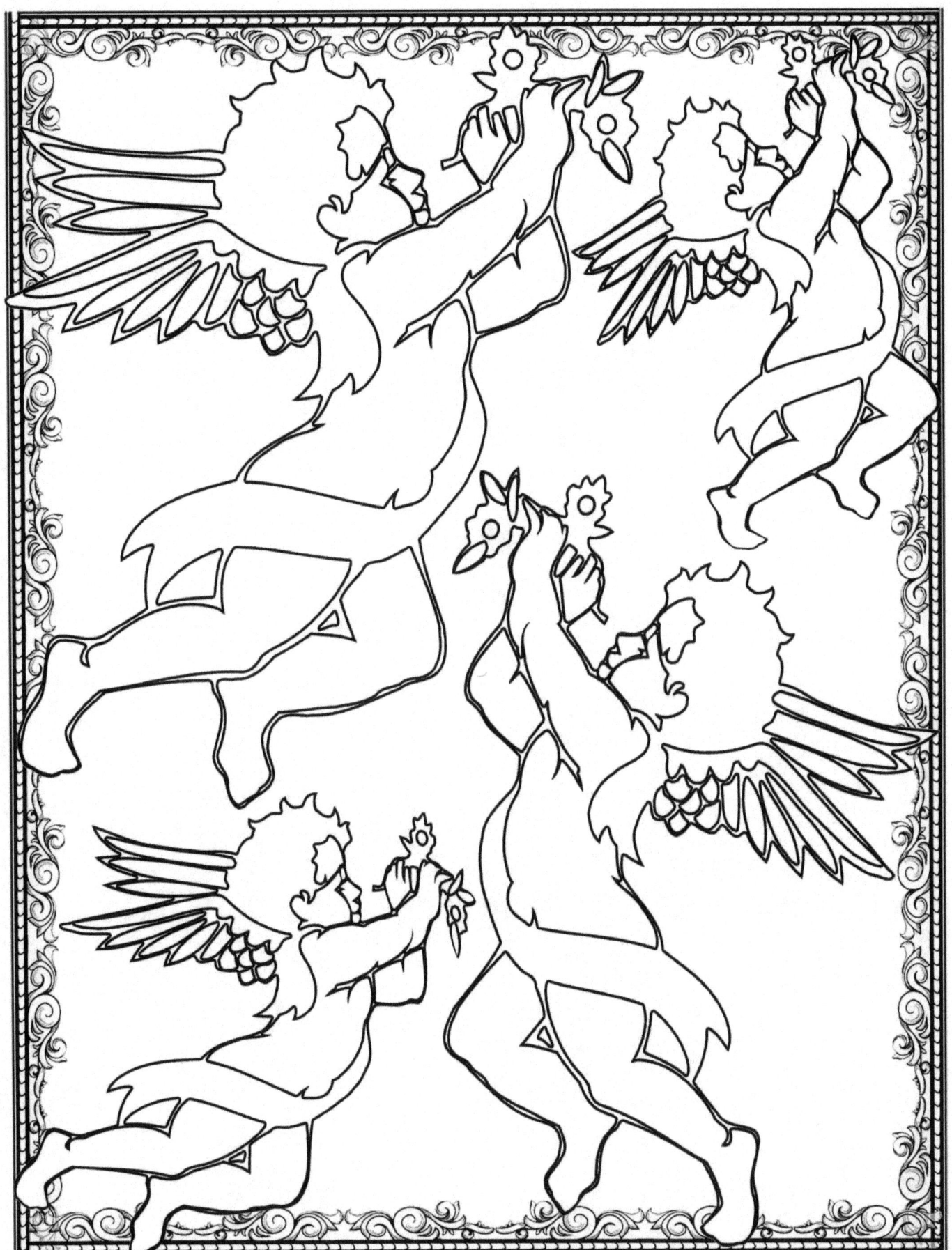

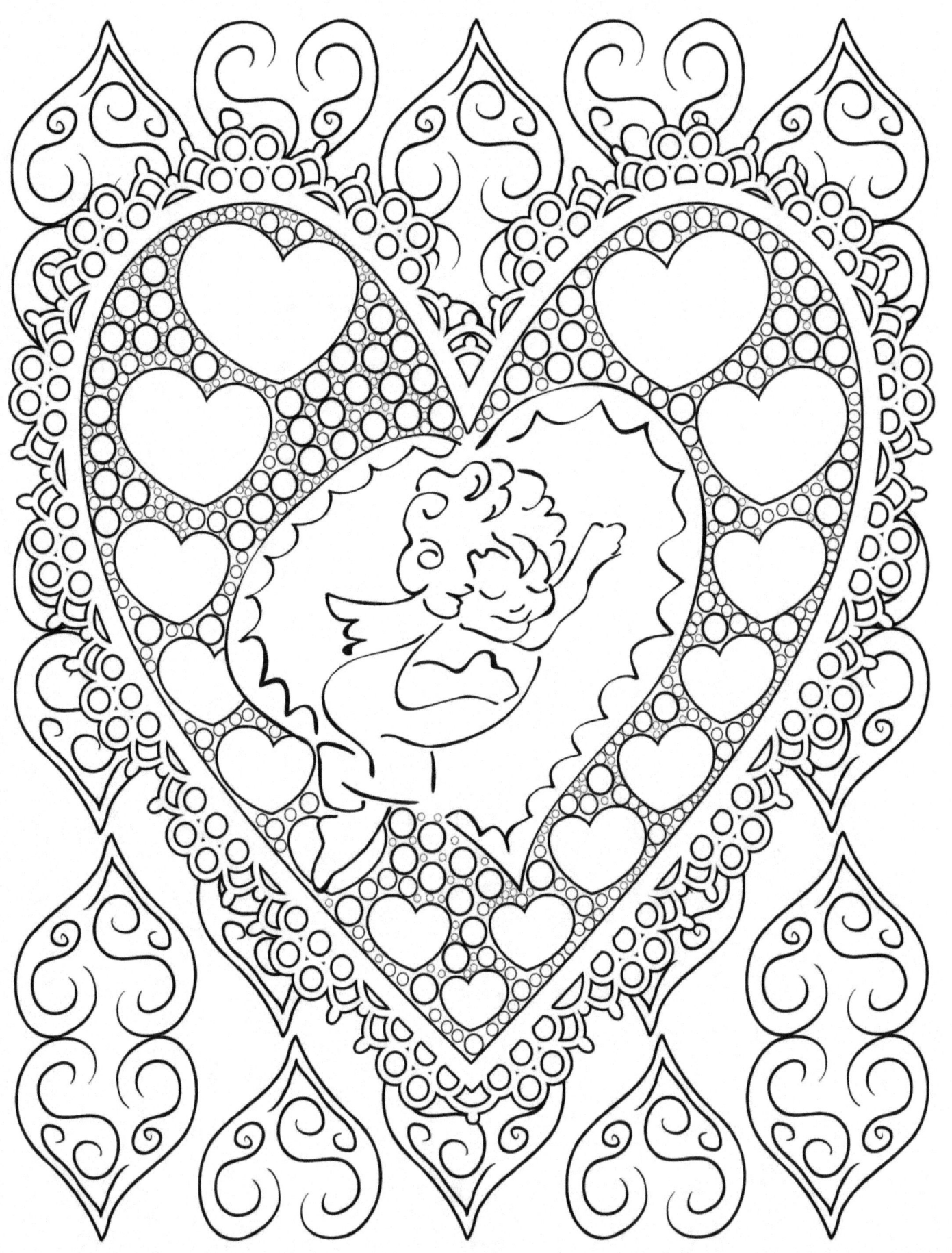

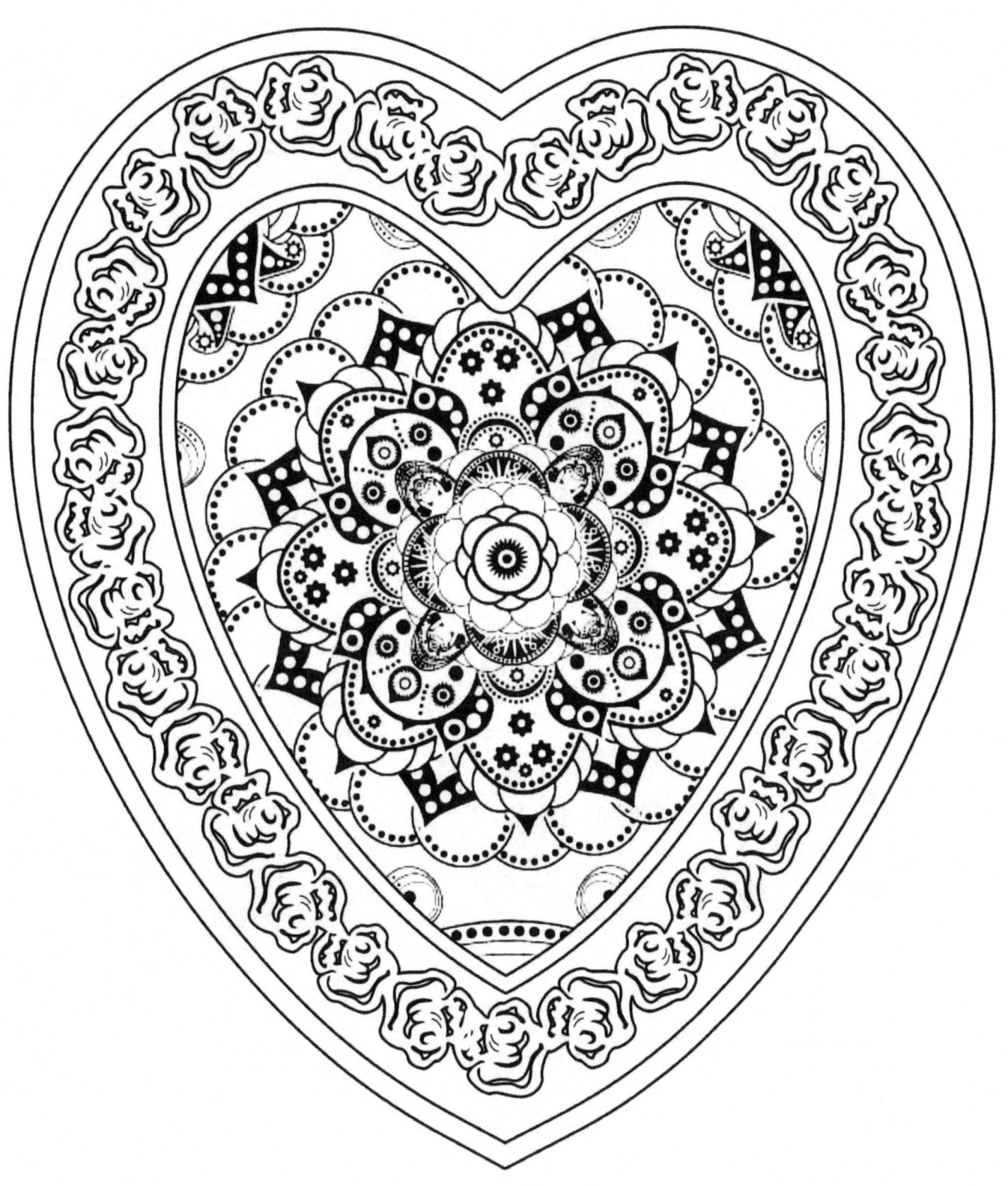

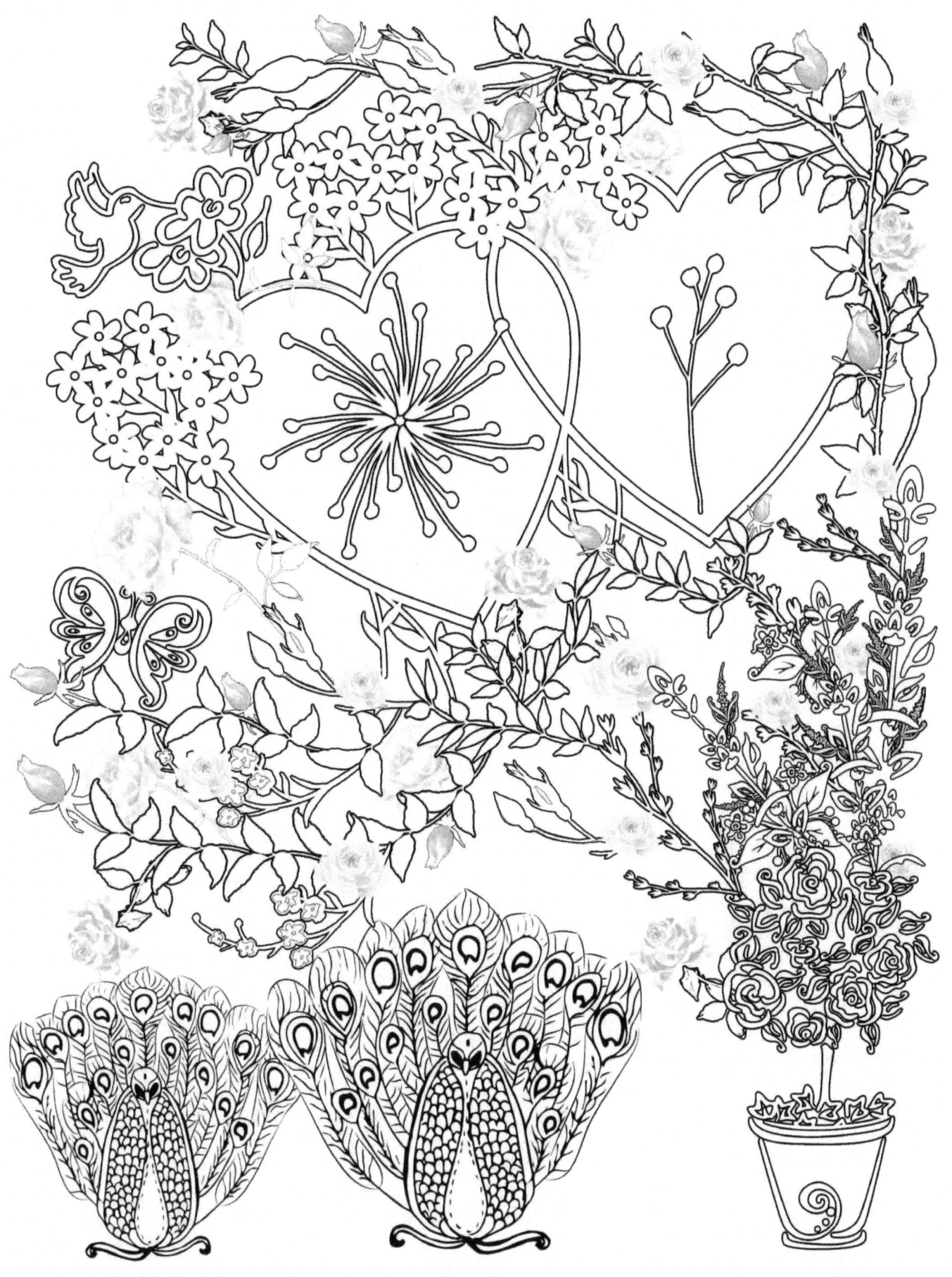

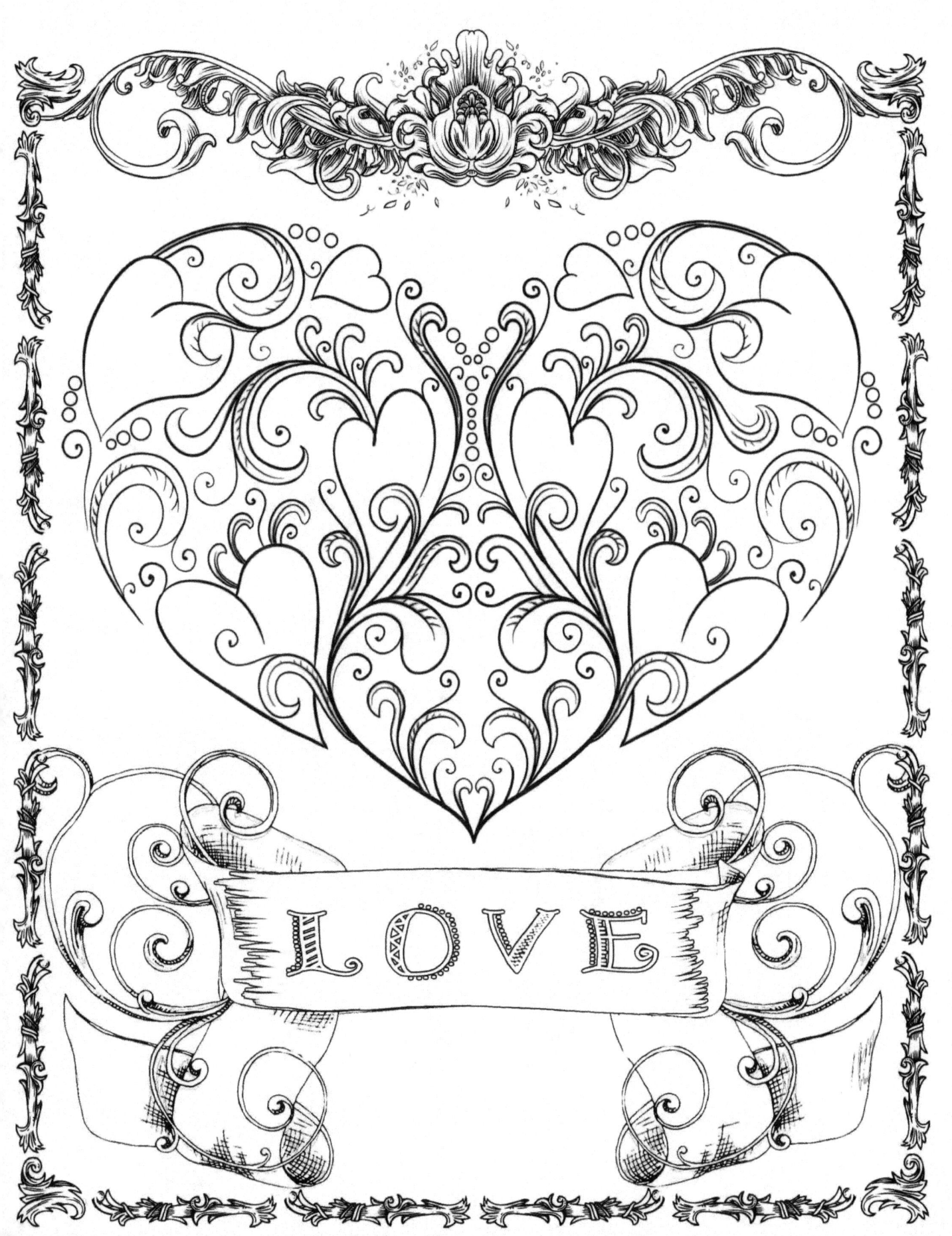

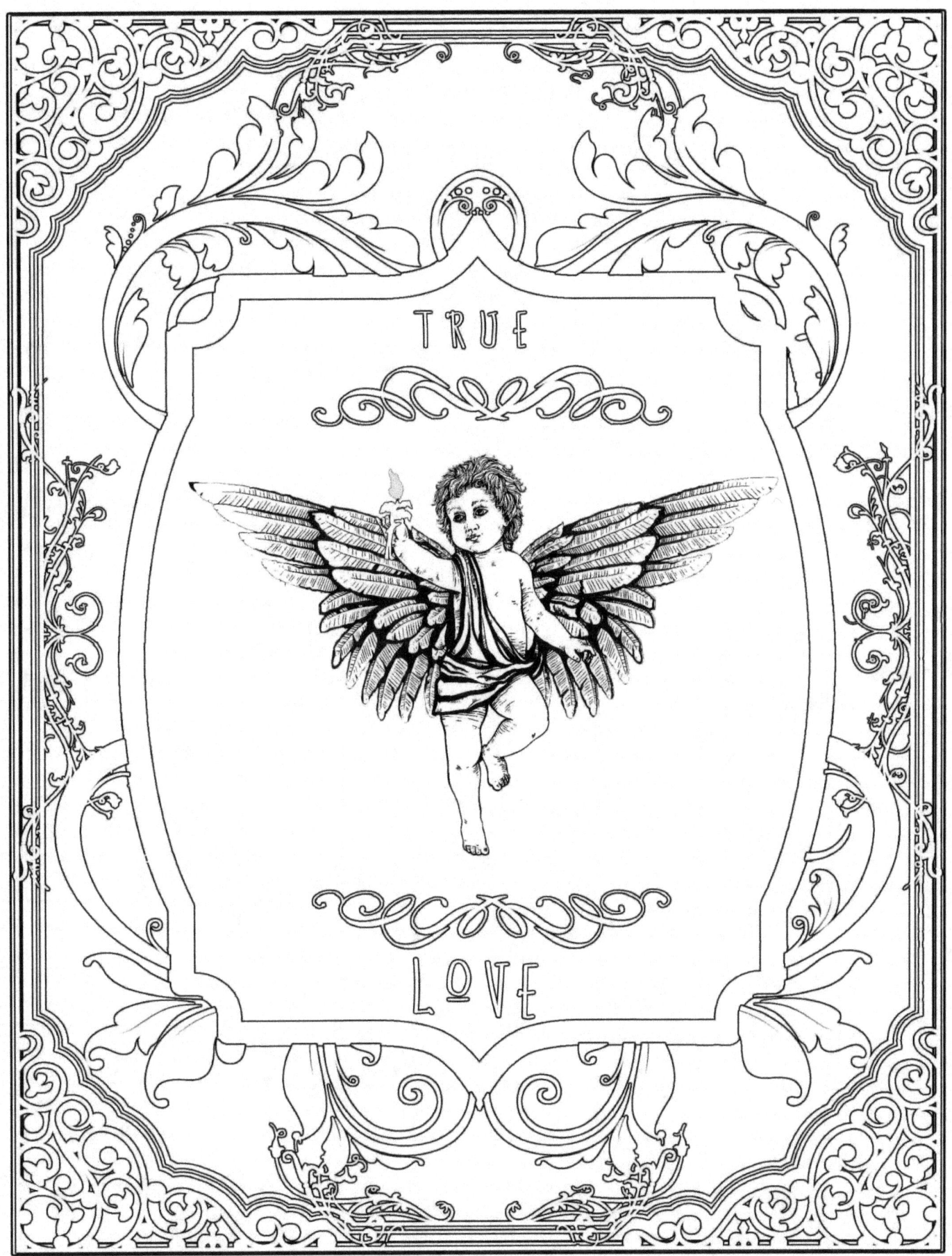

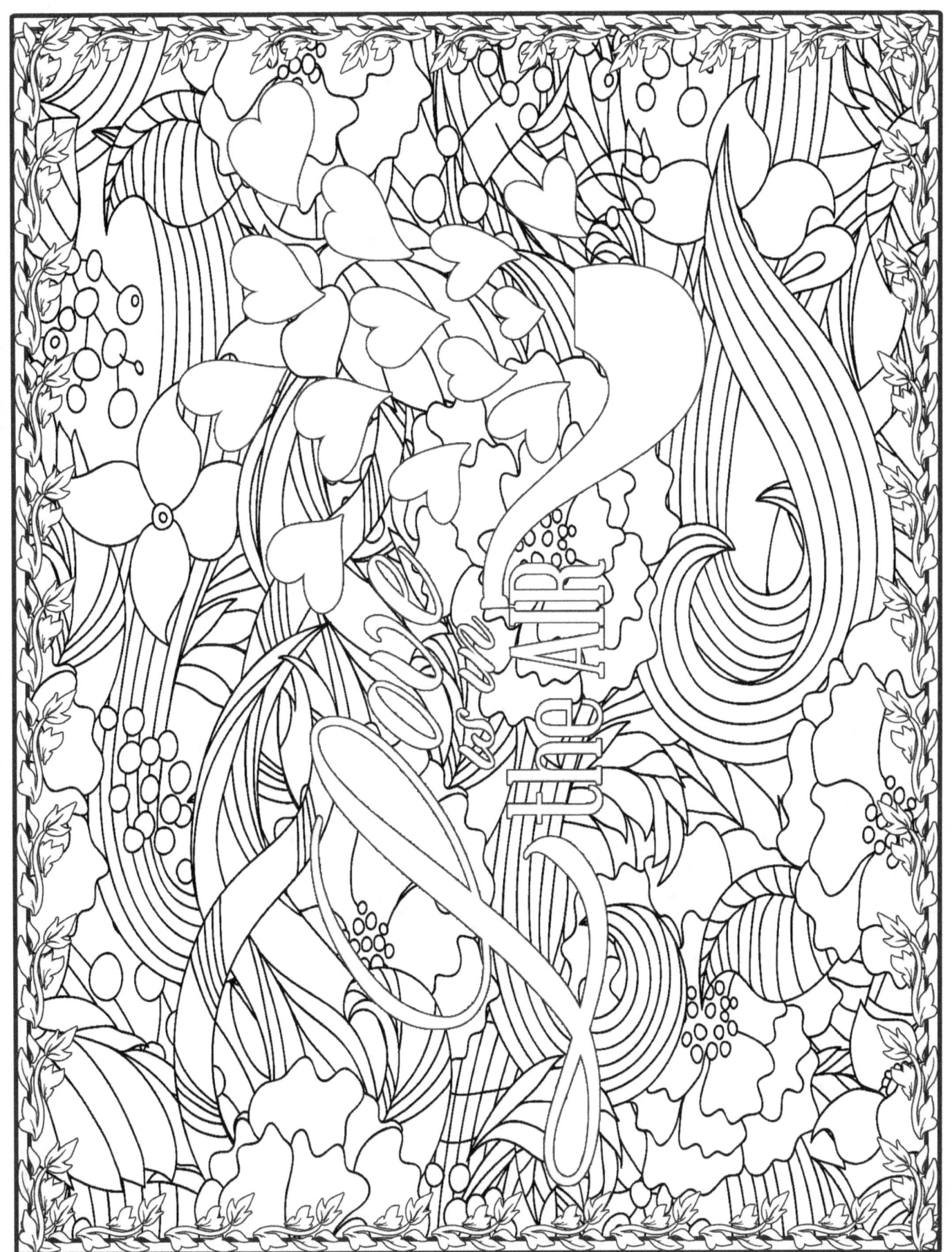

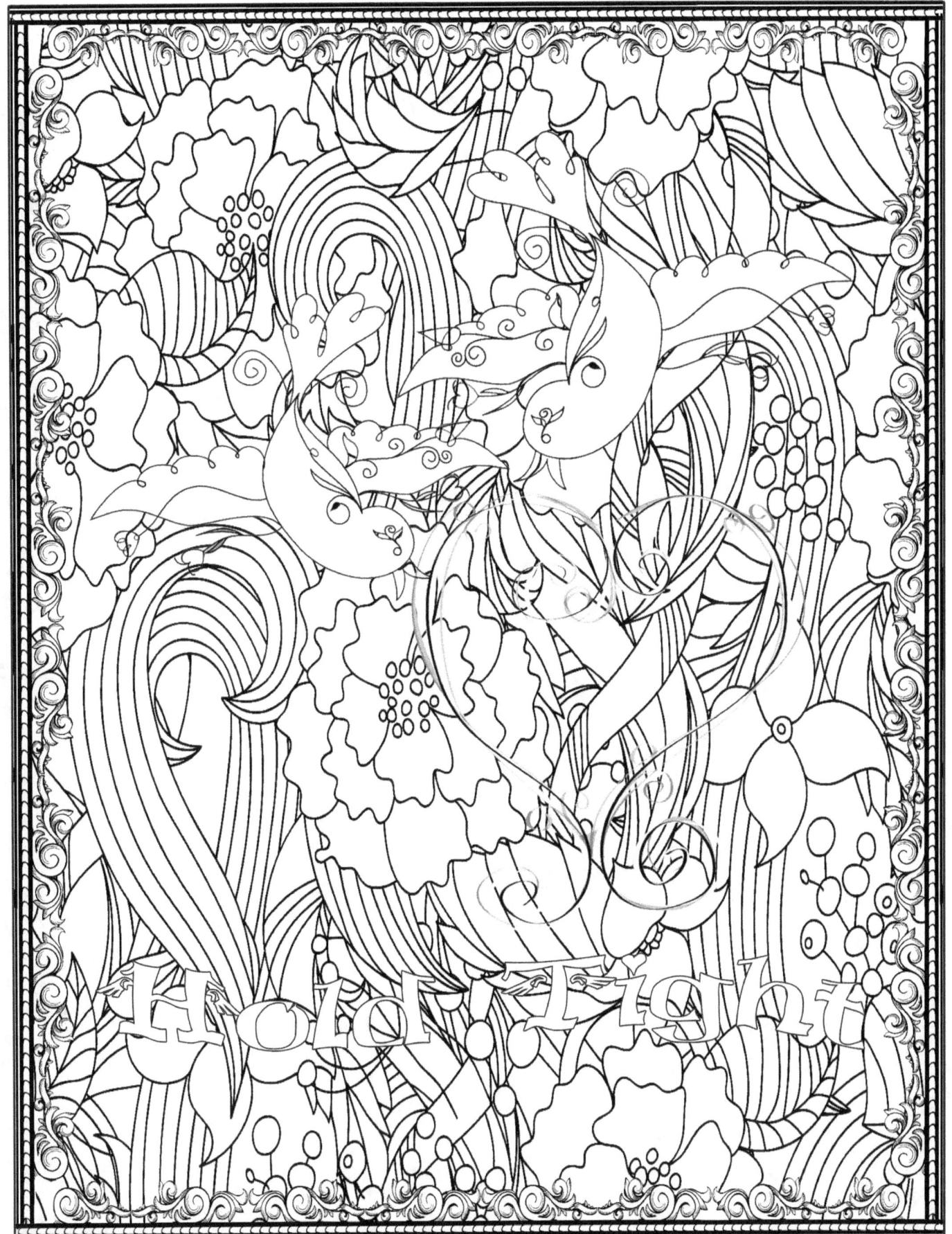

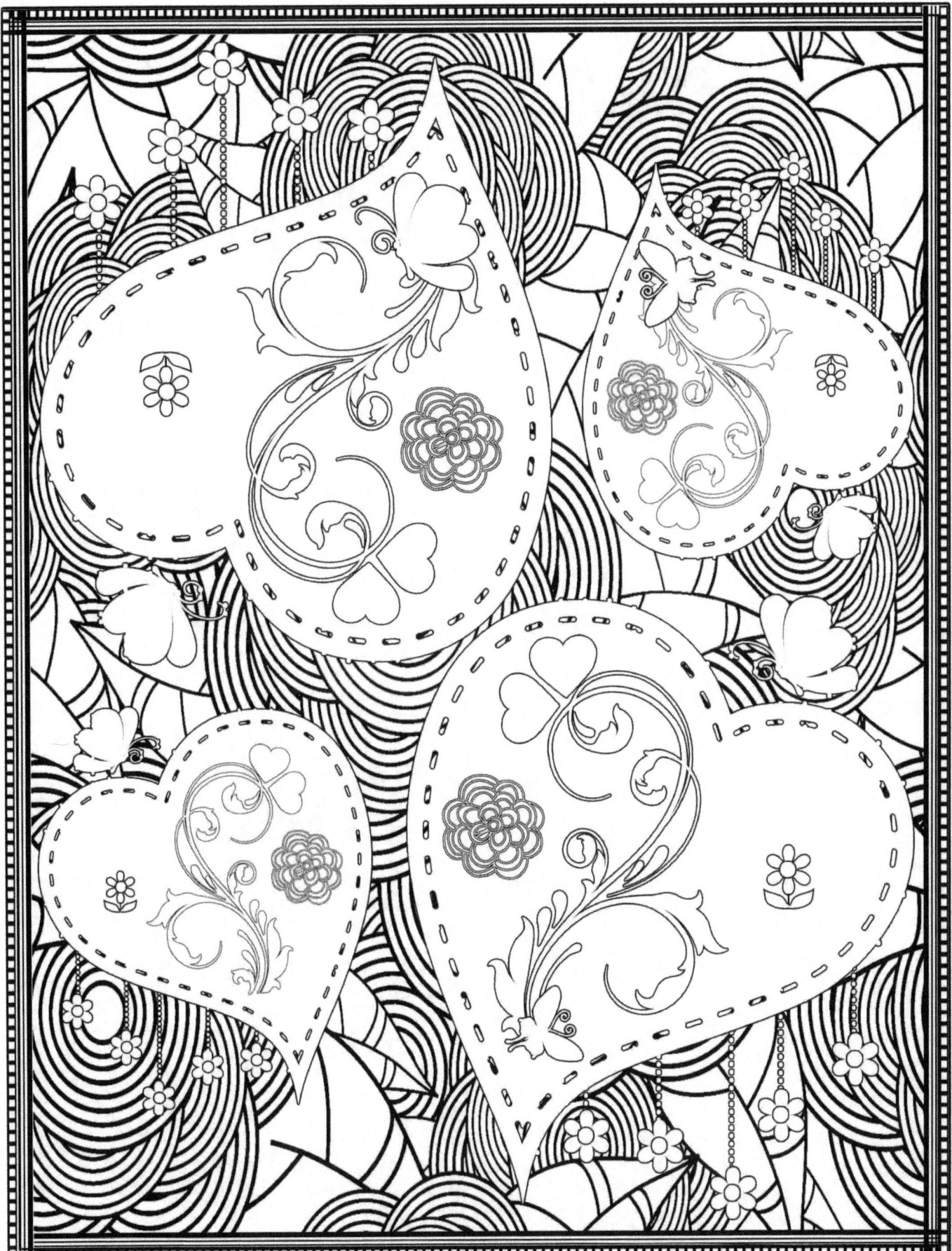

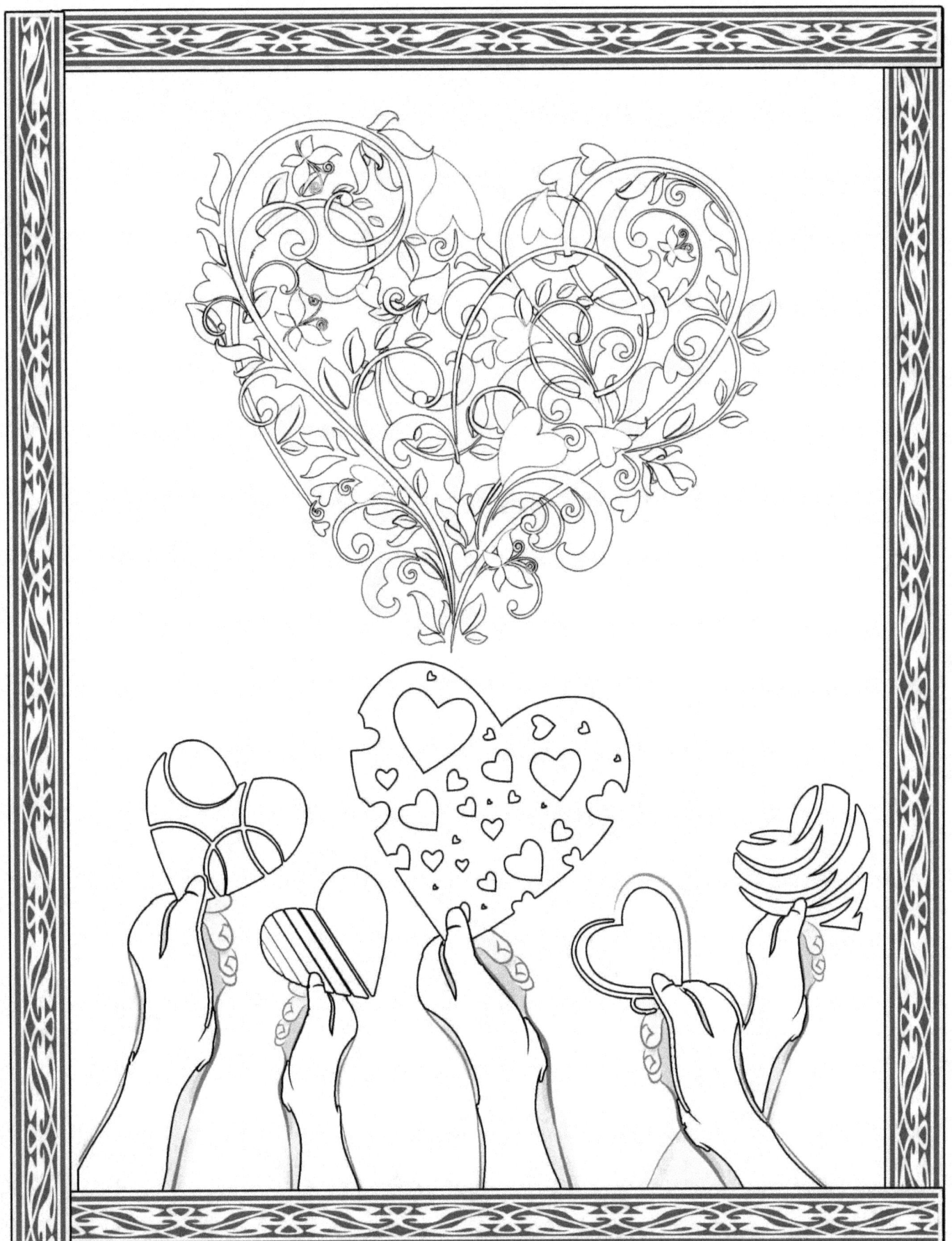

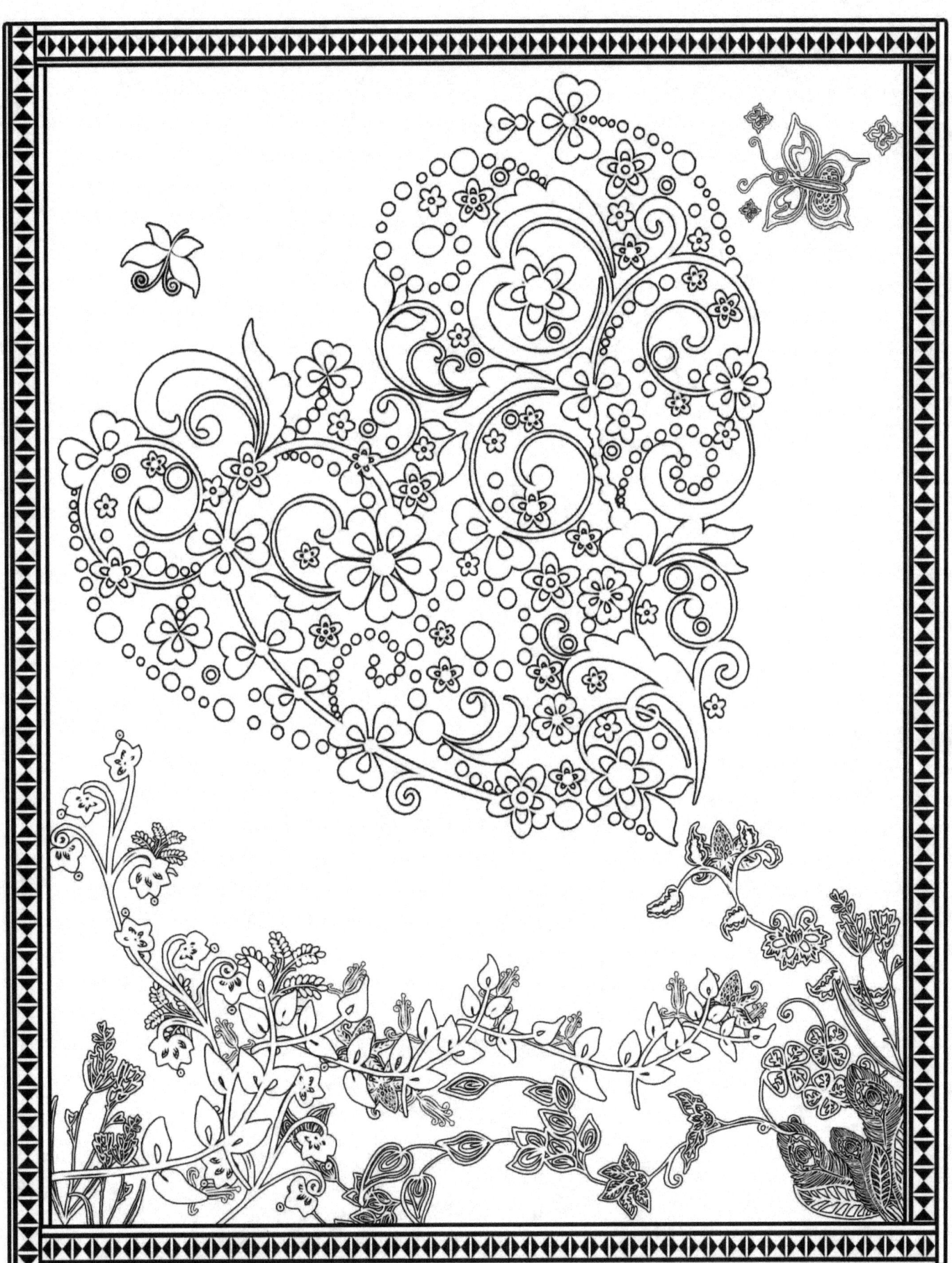

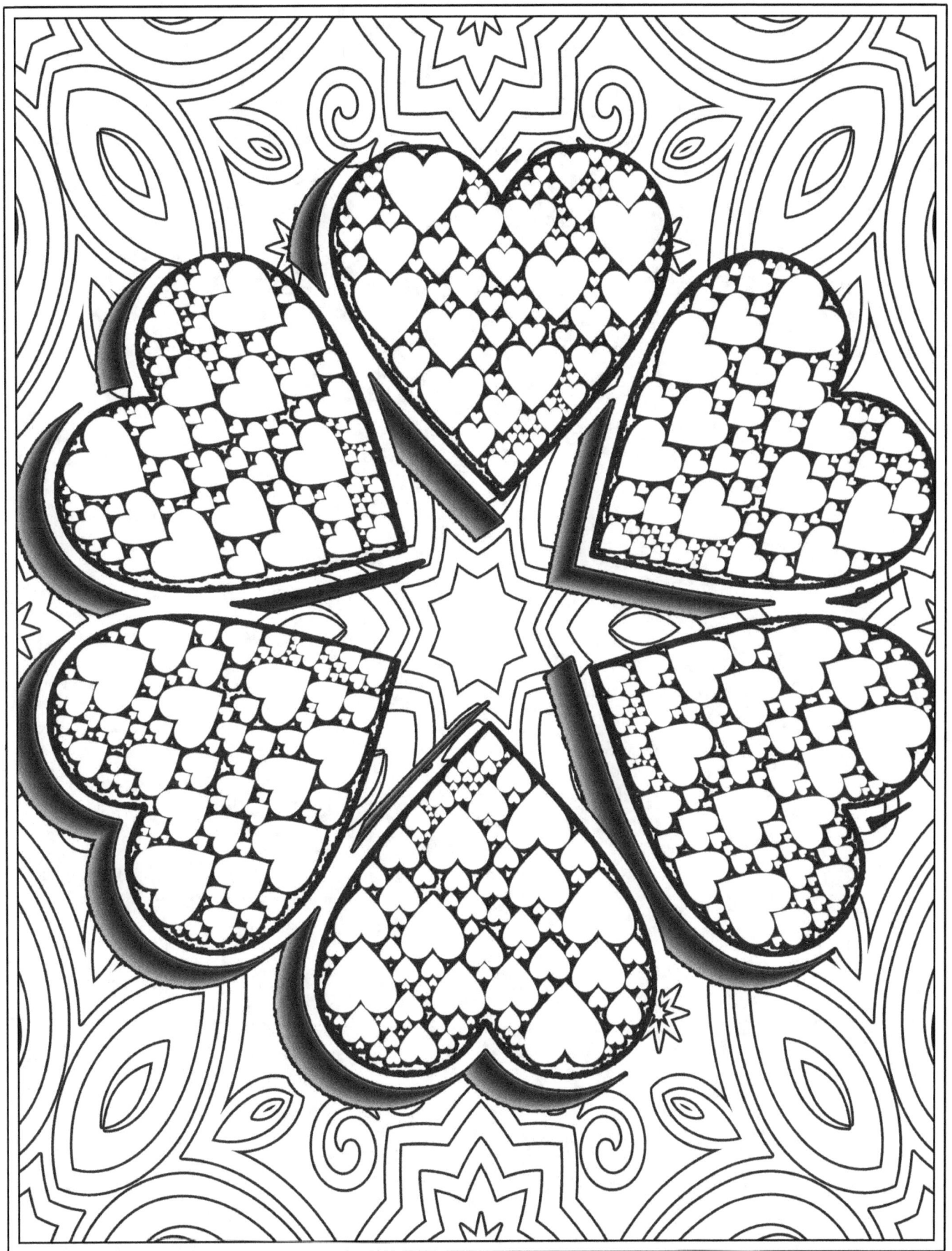

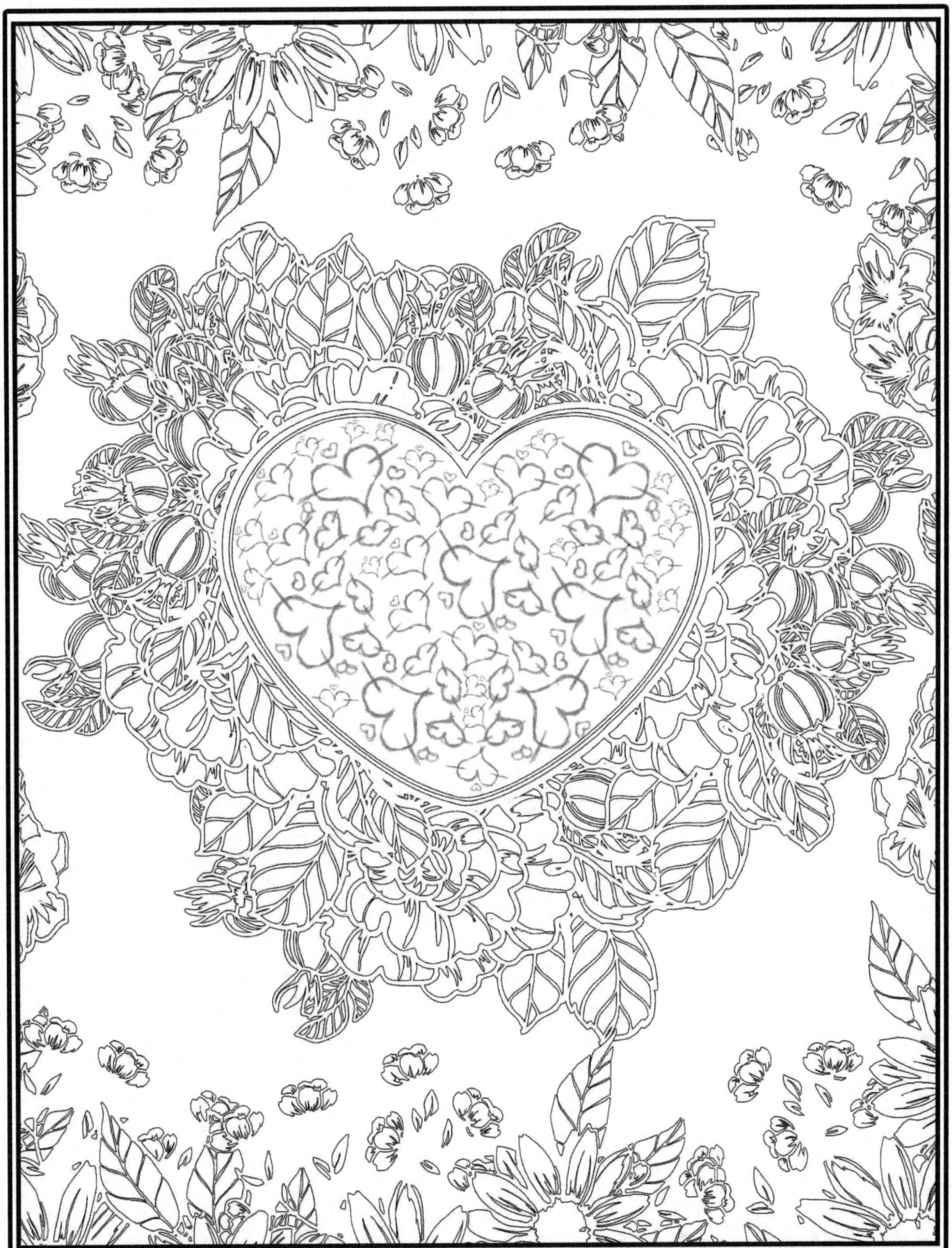

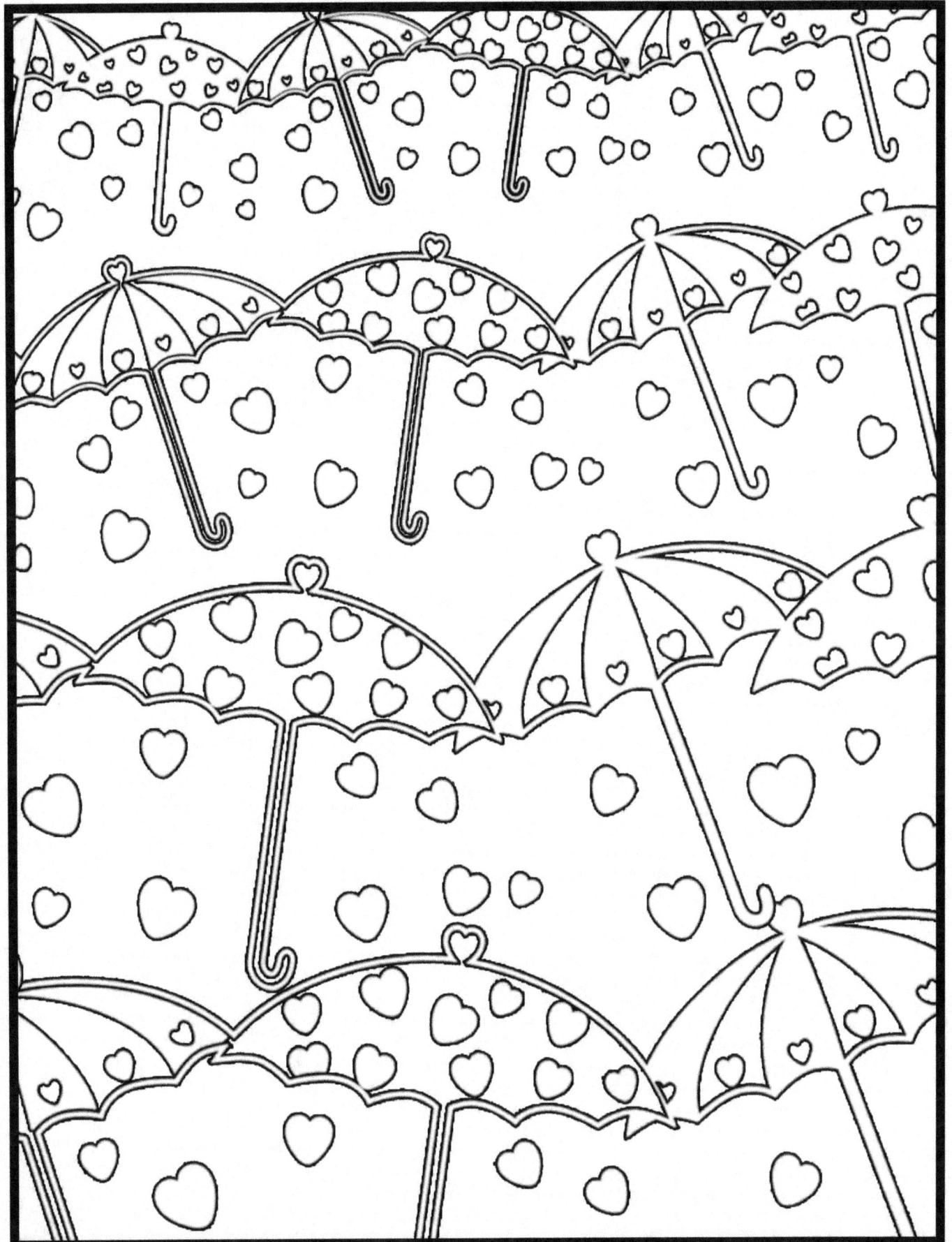

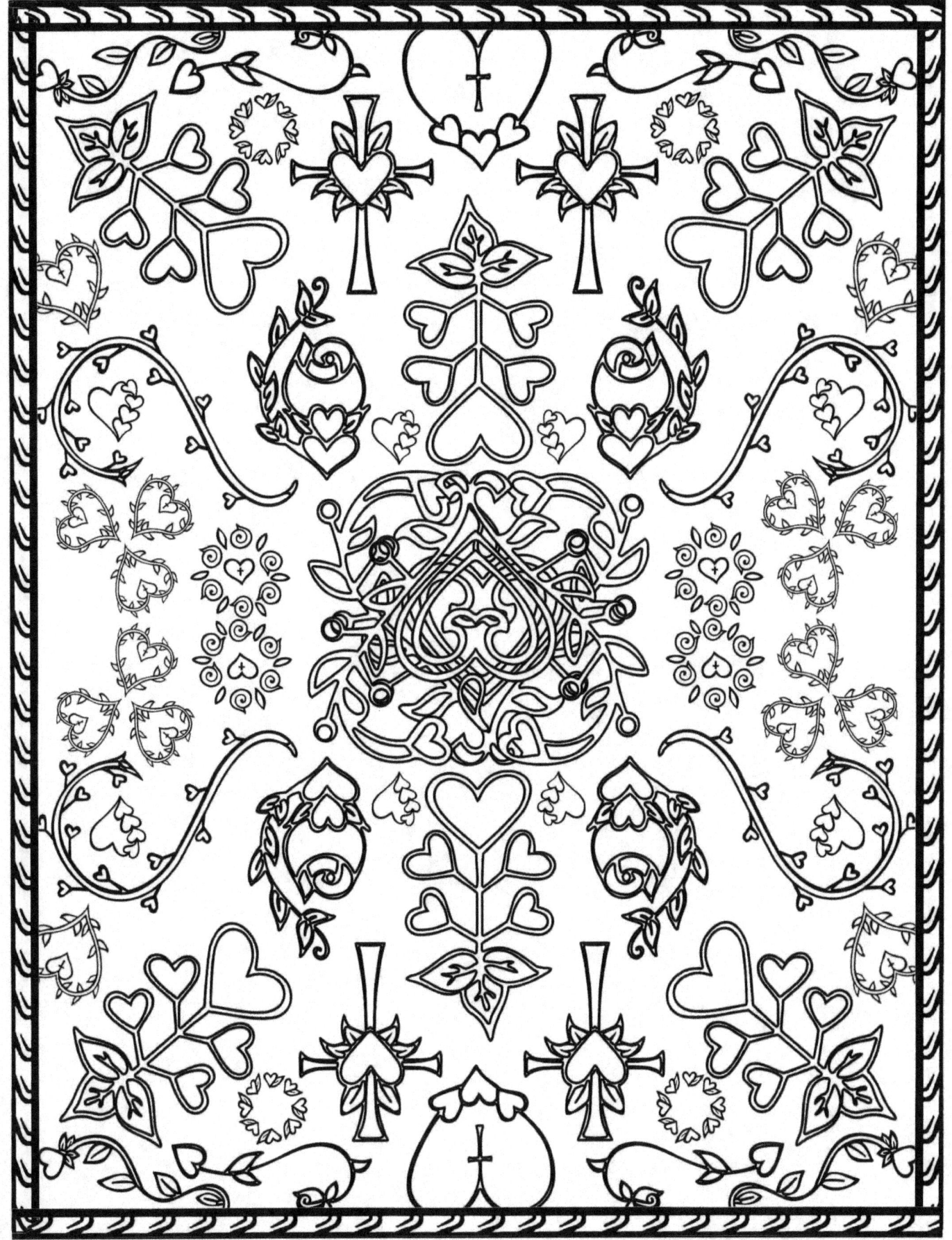

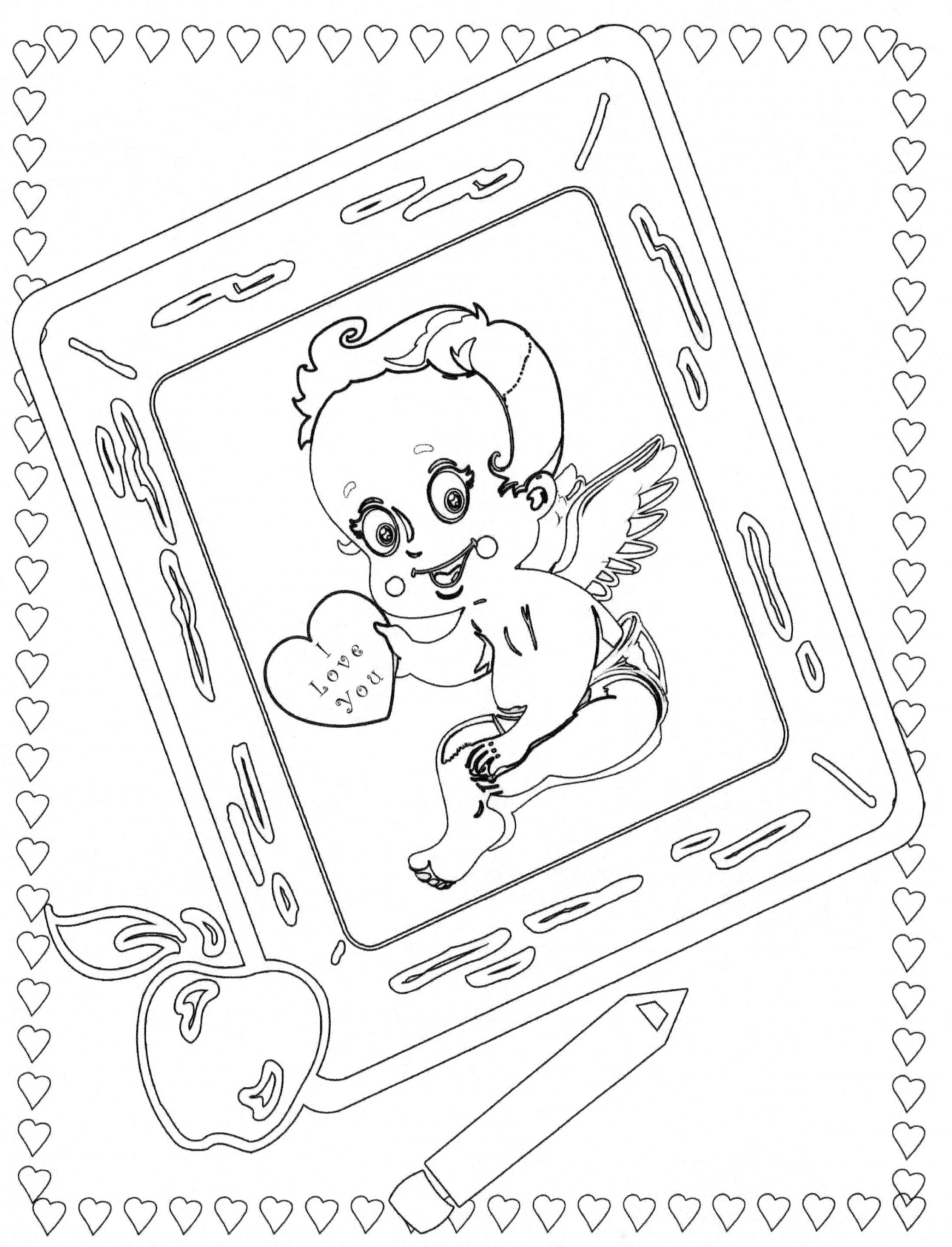

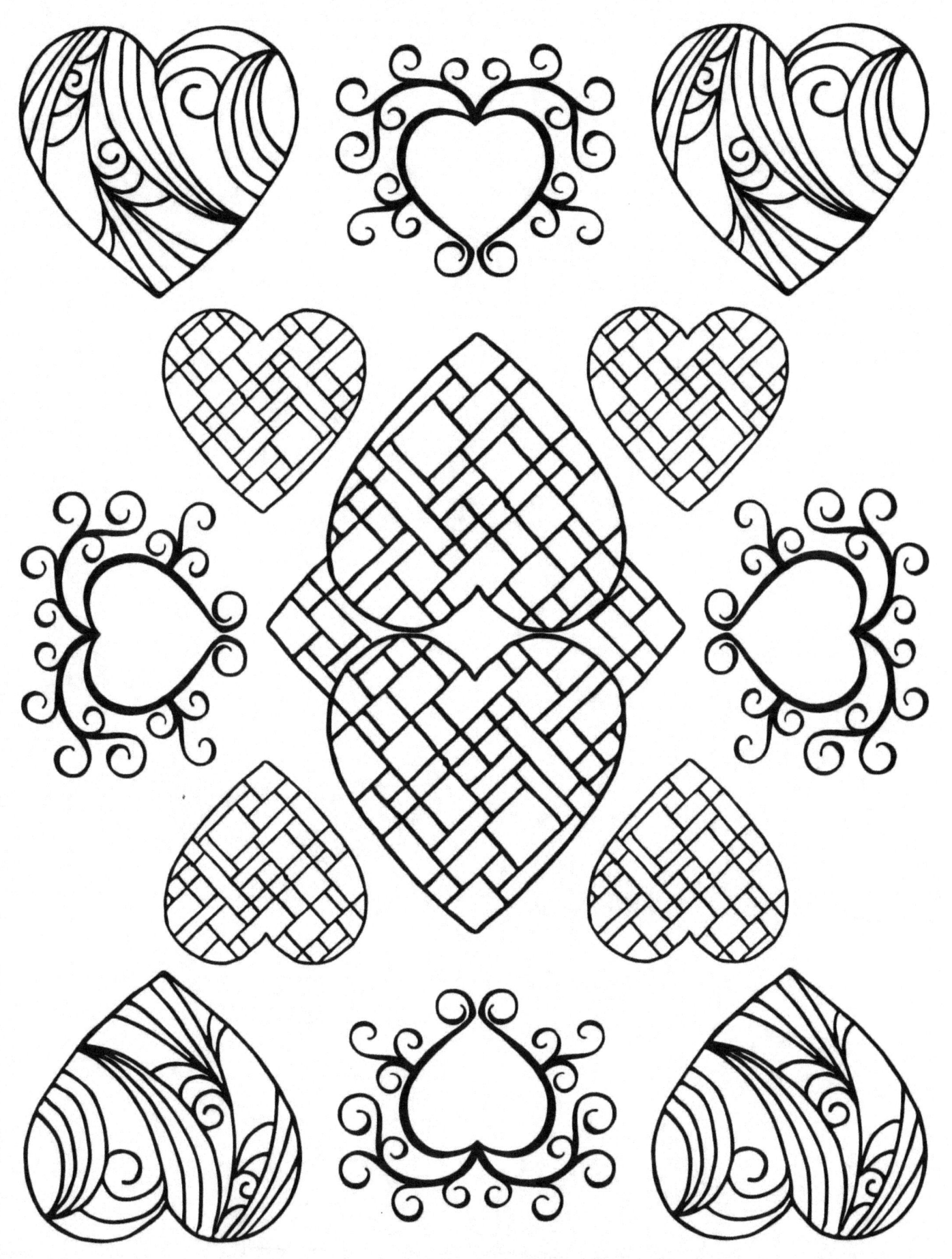

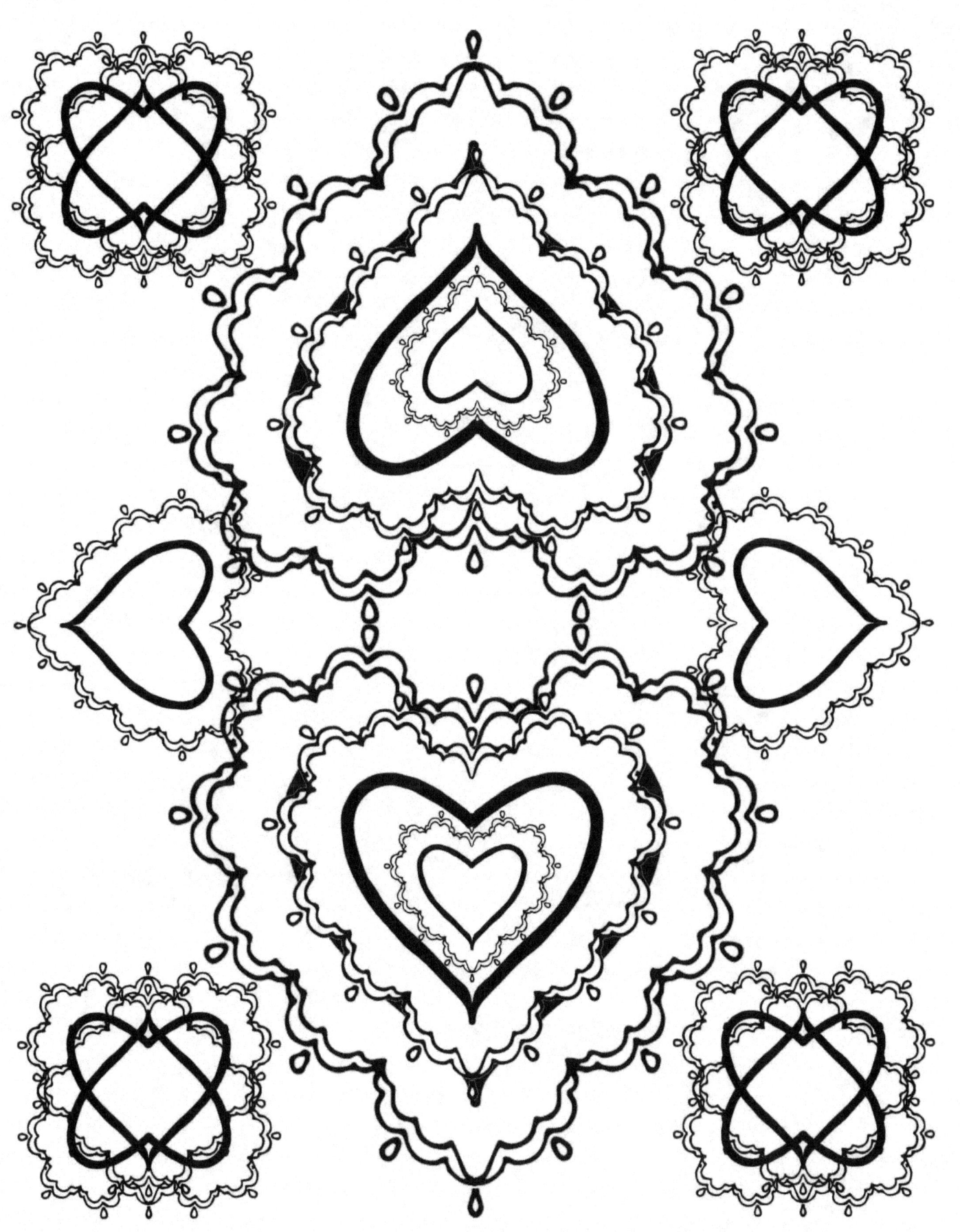

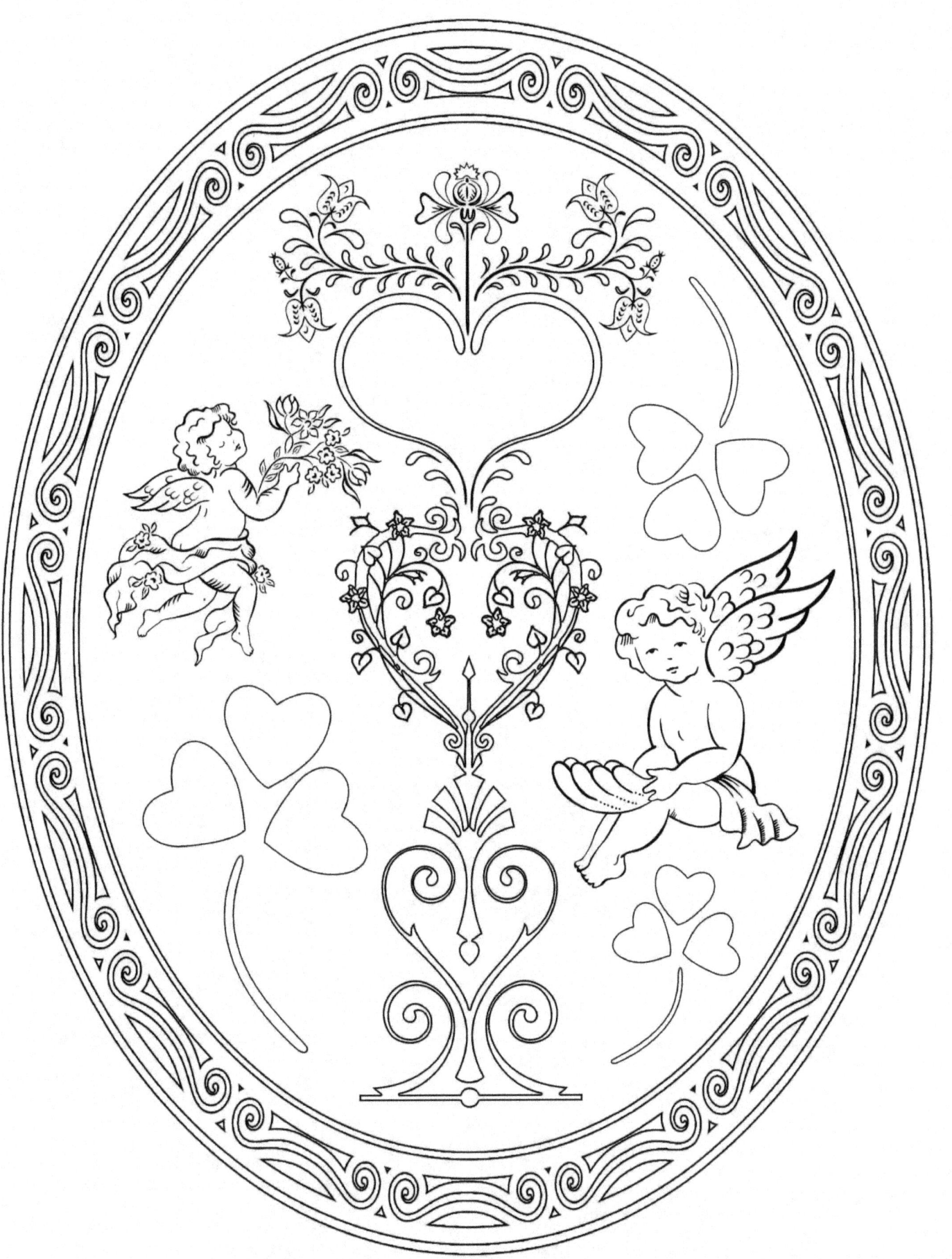

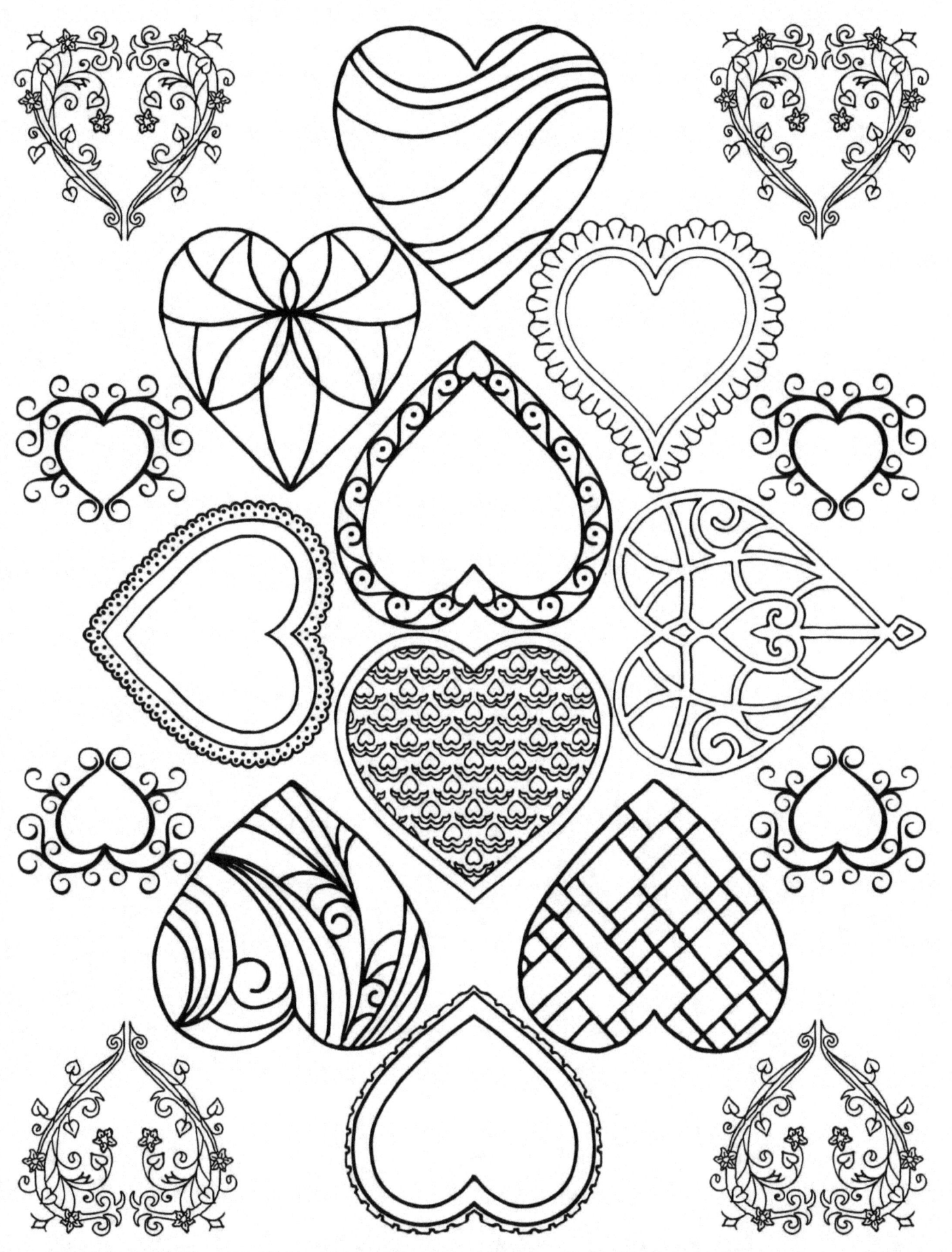

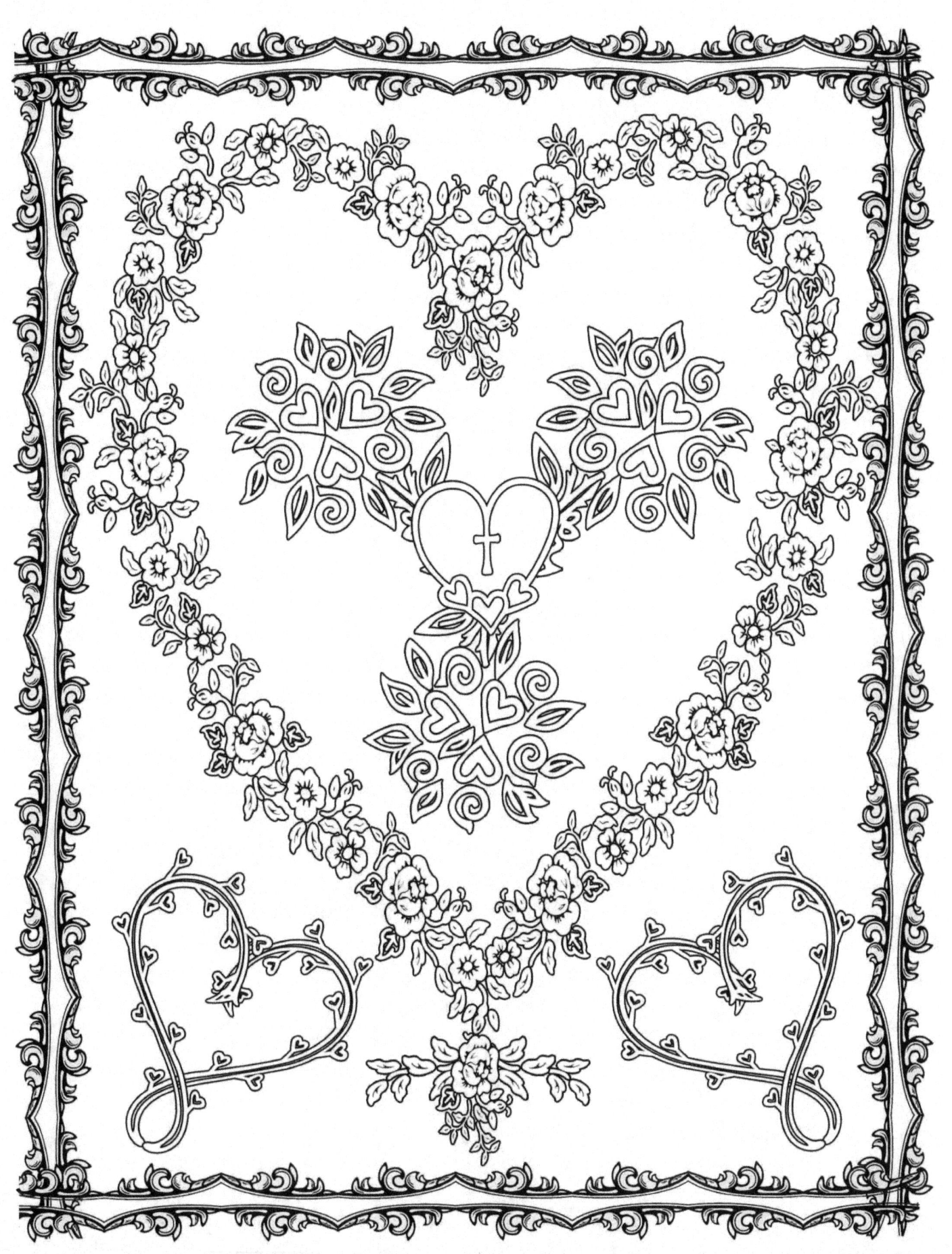

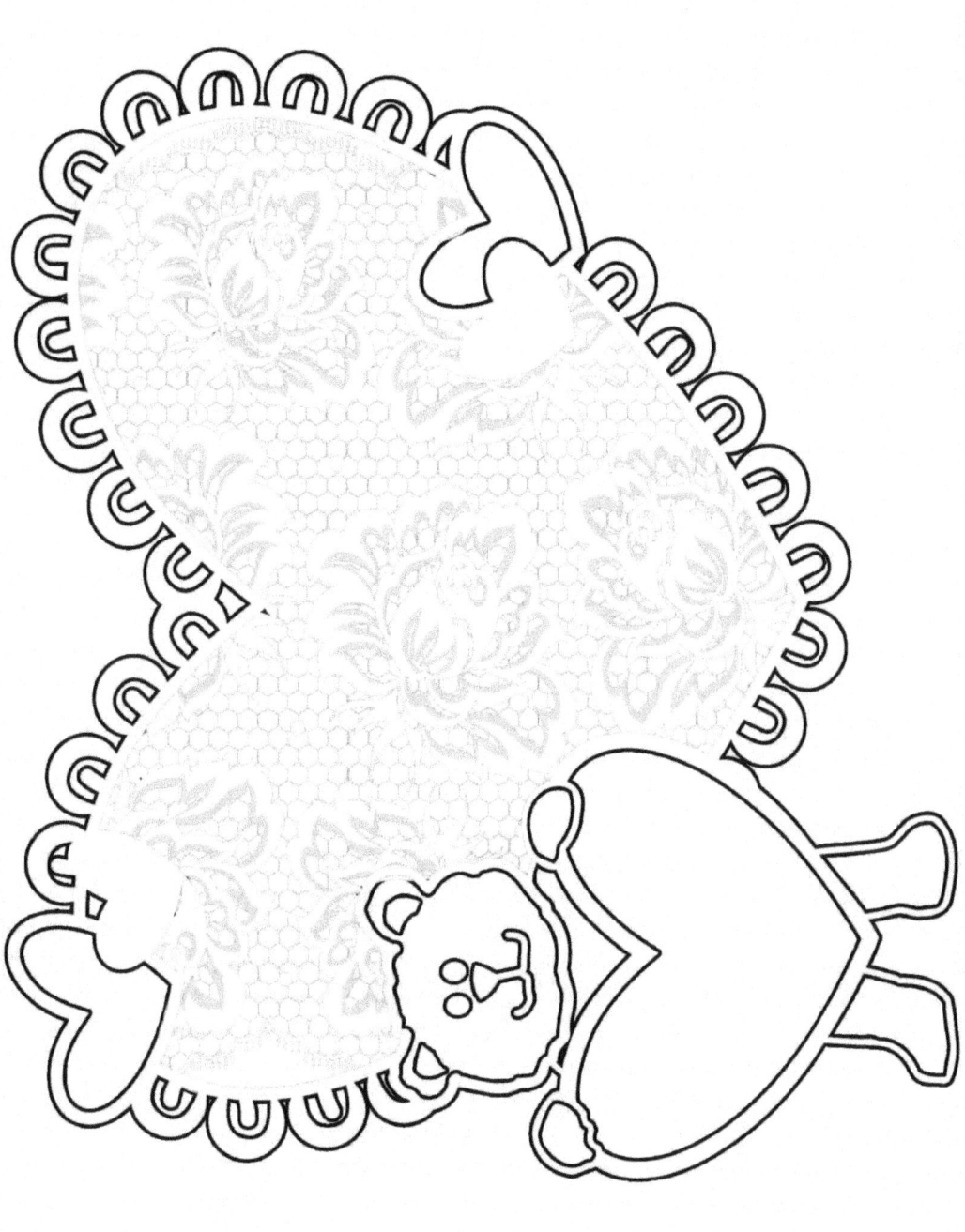

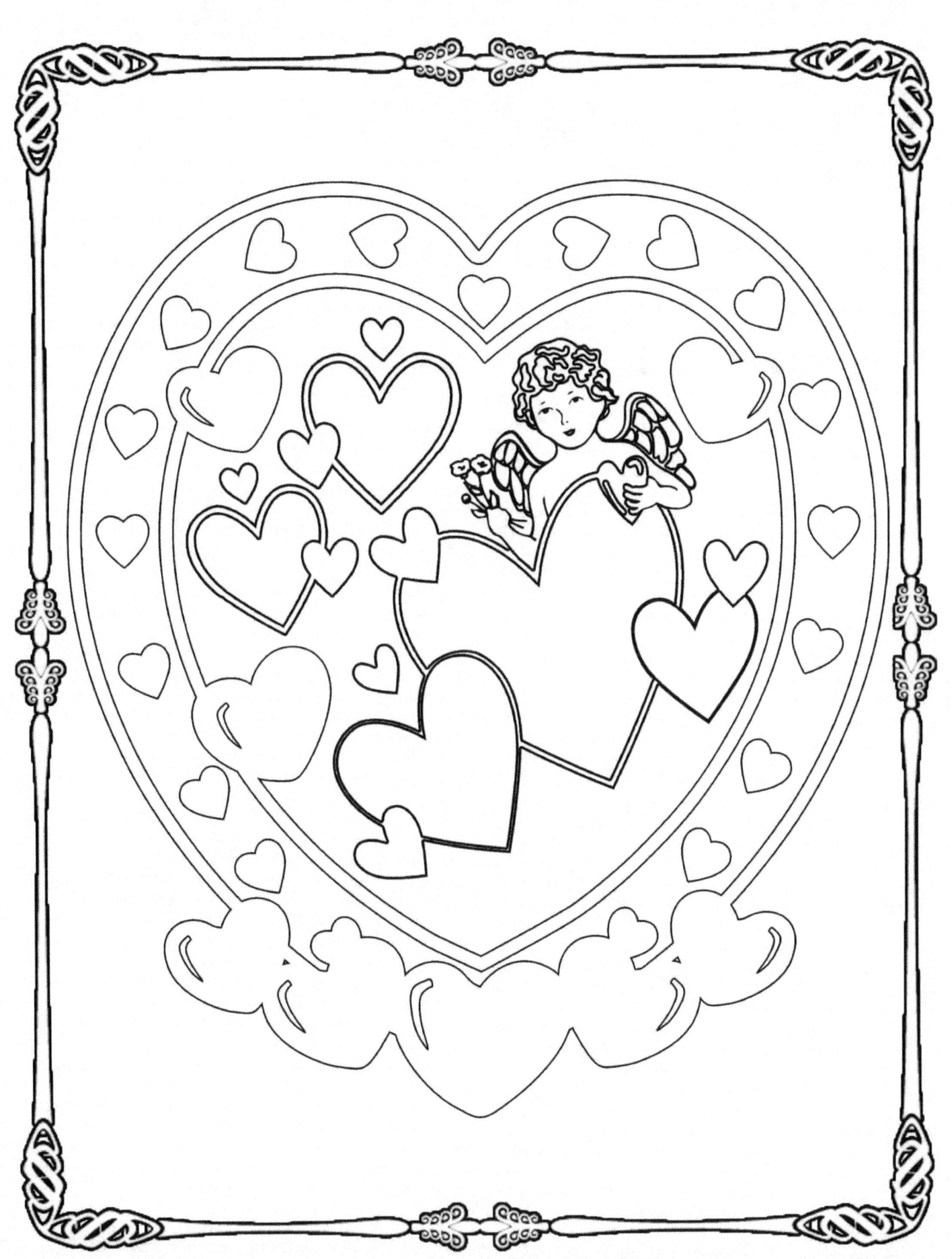

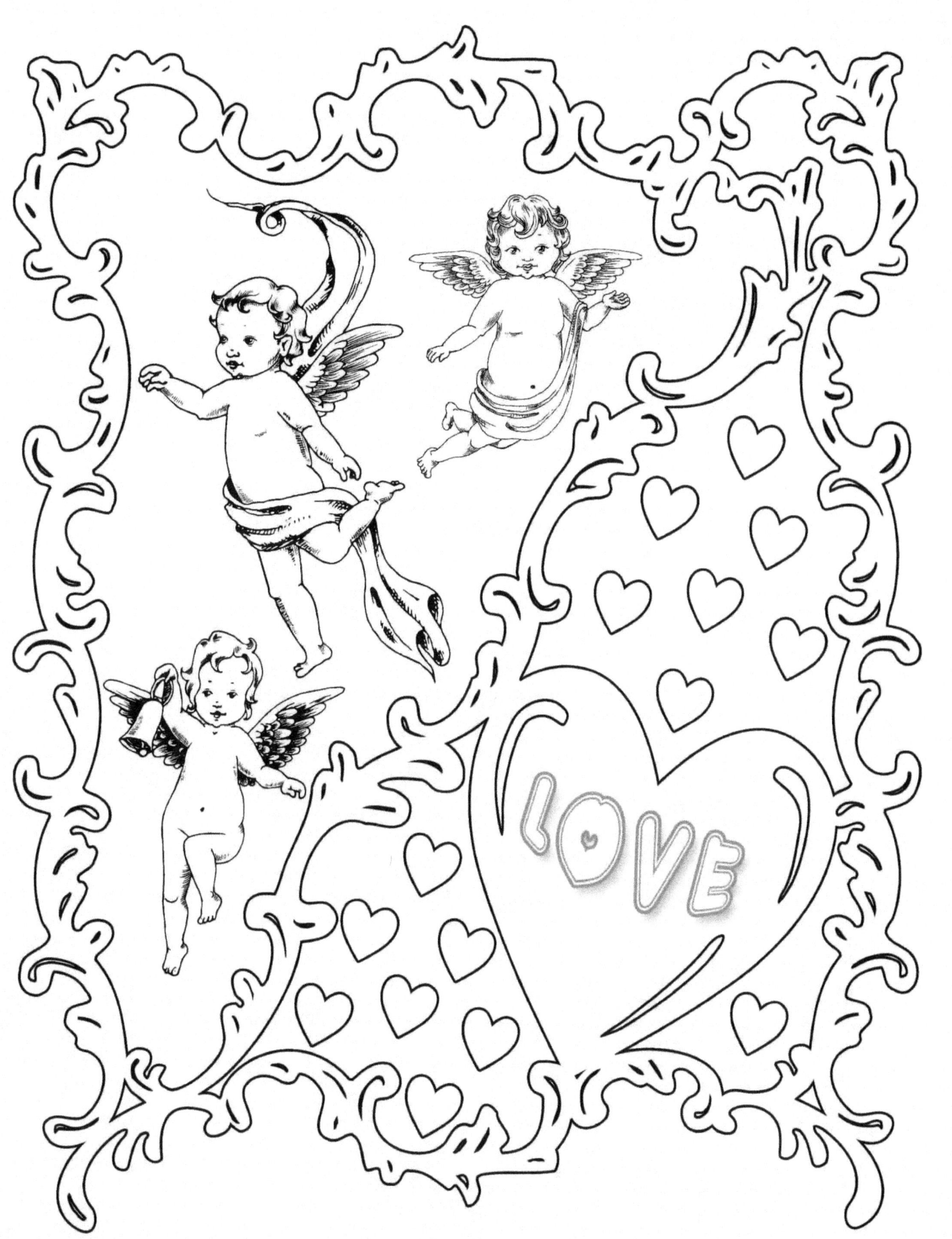

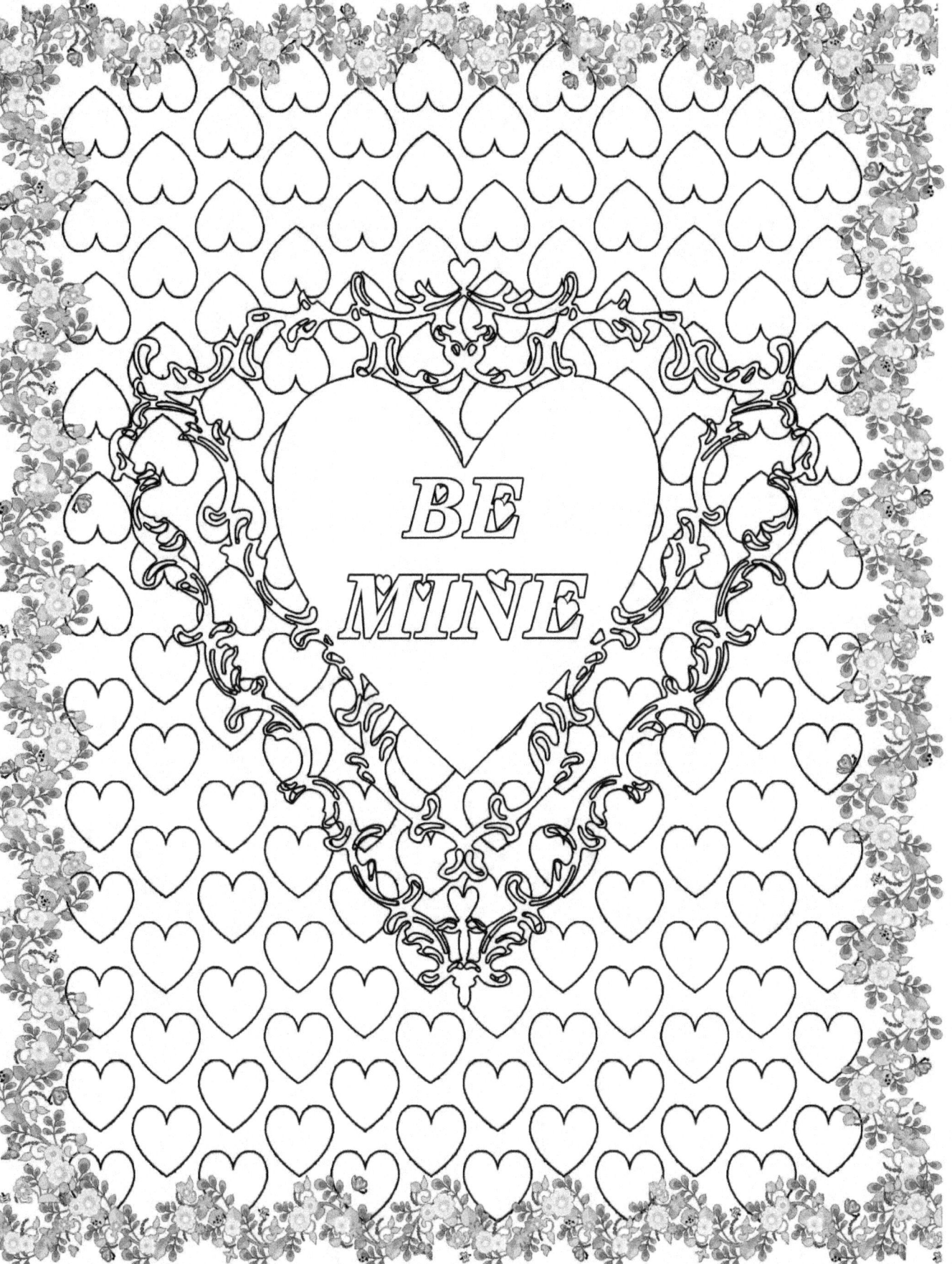

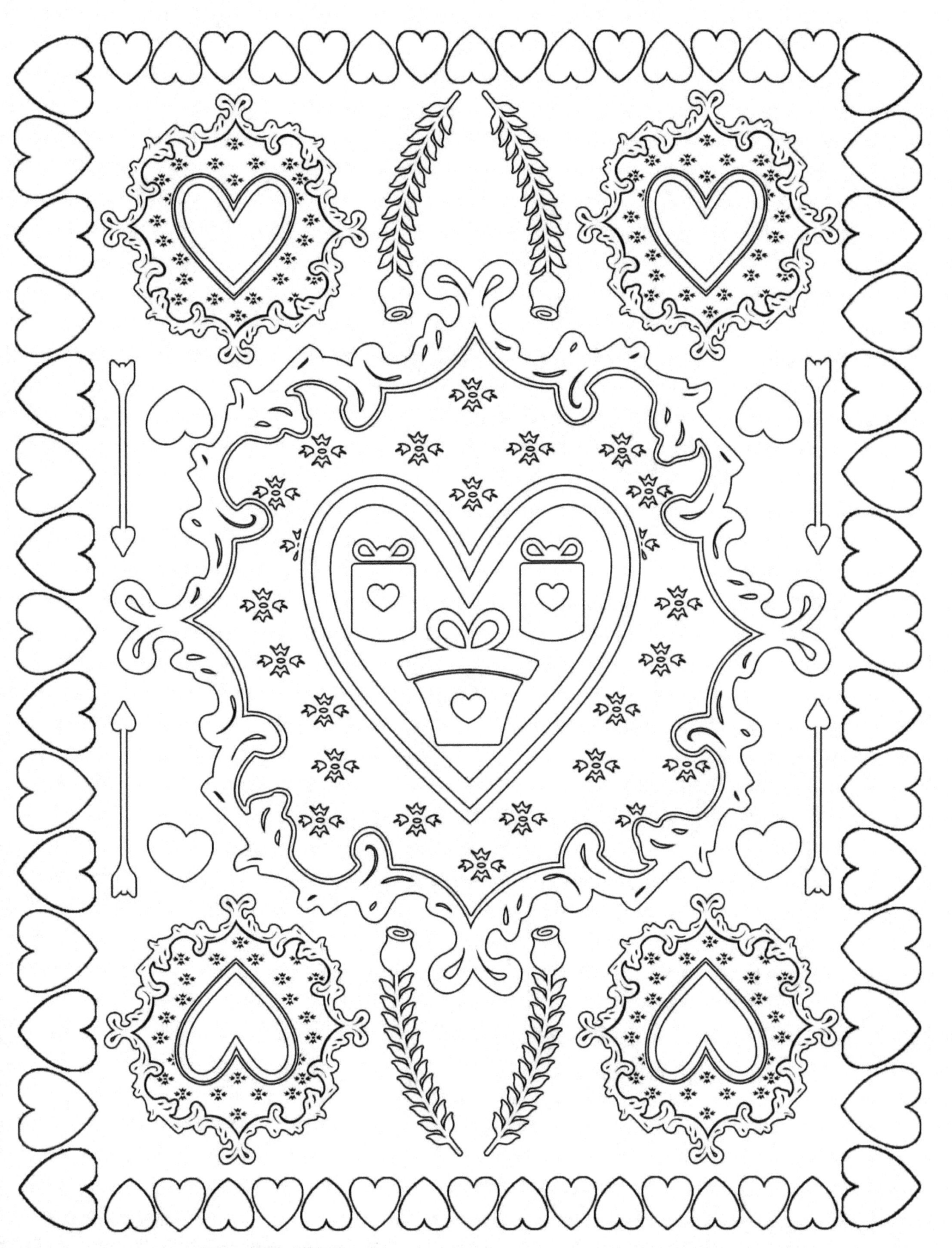

HAPPY VALENTINE'S DAY

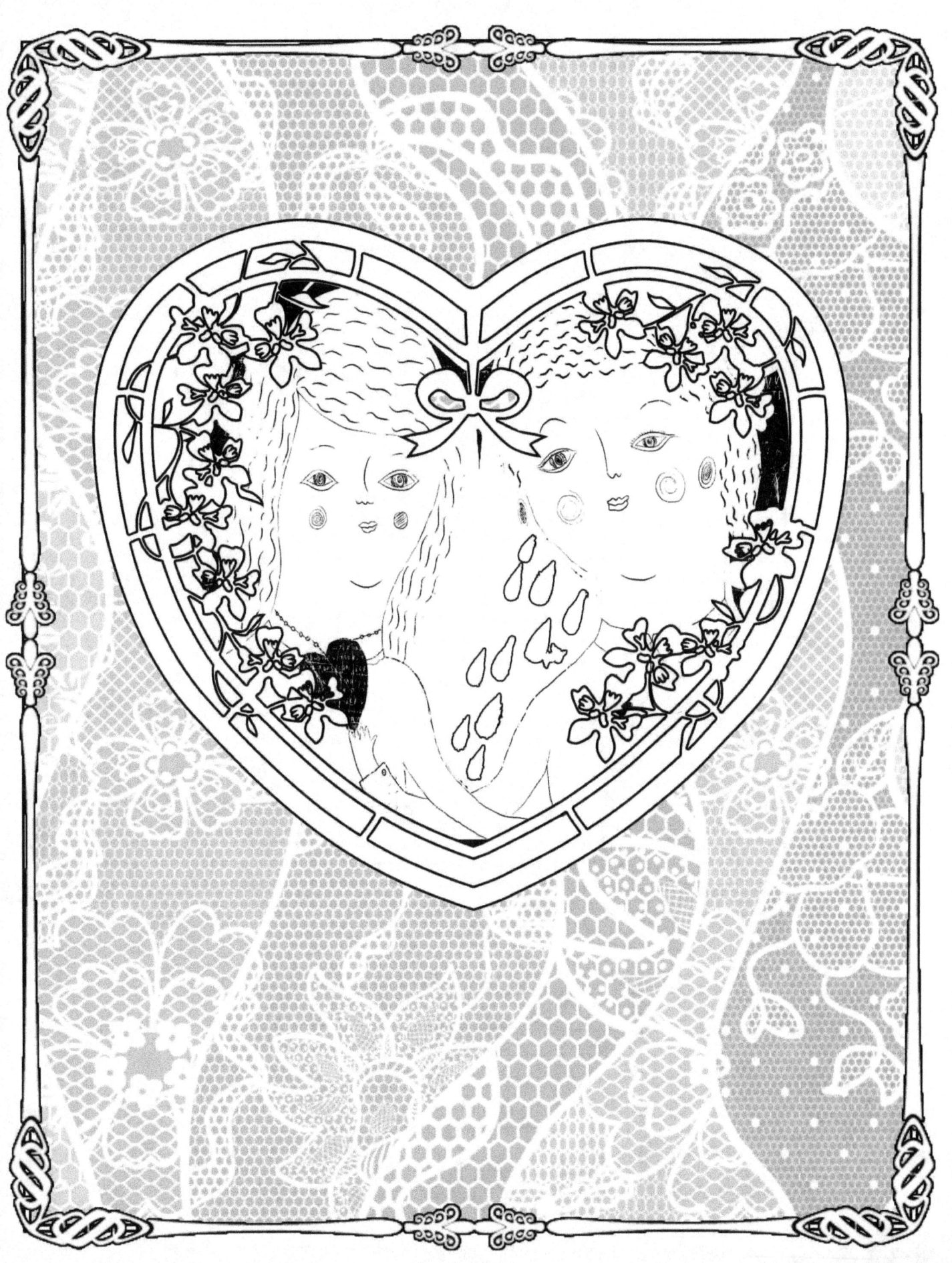

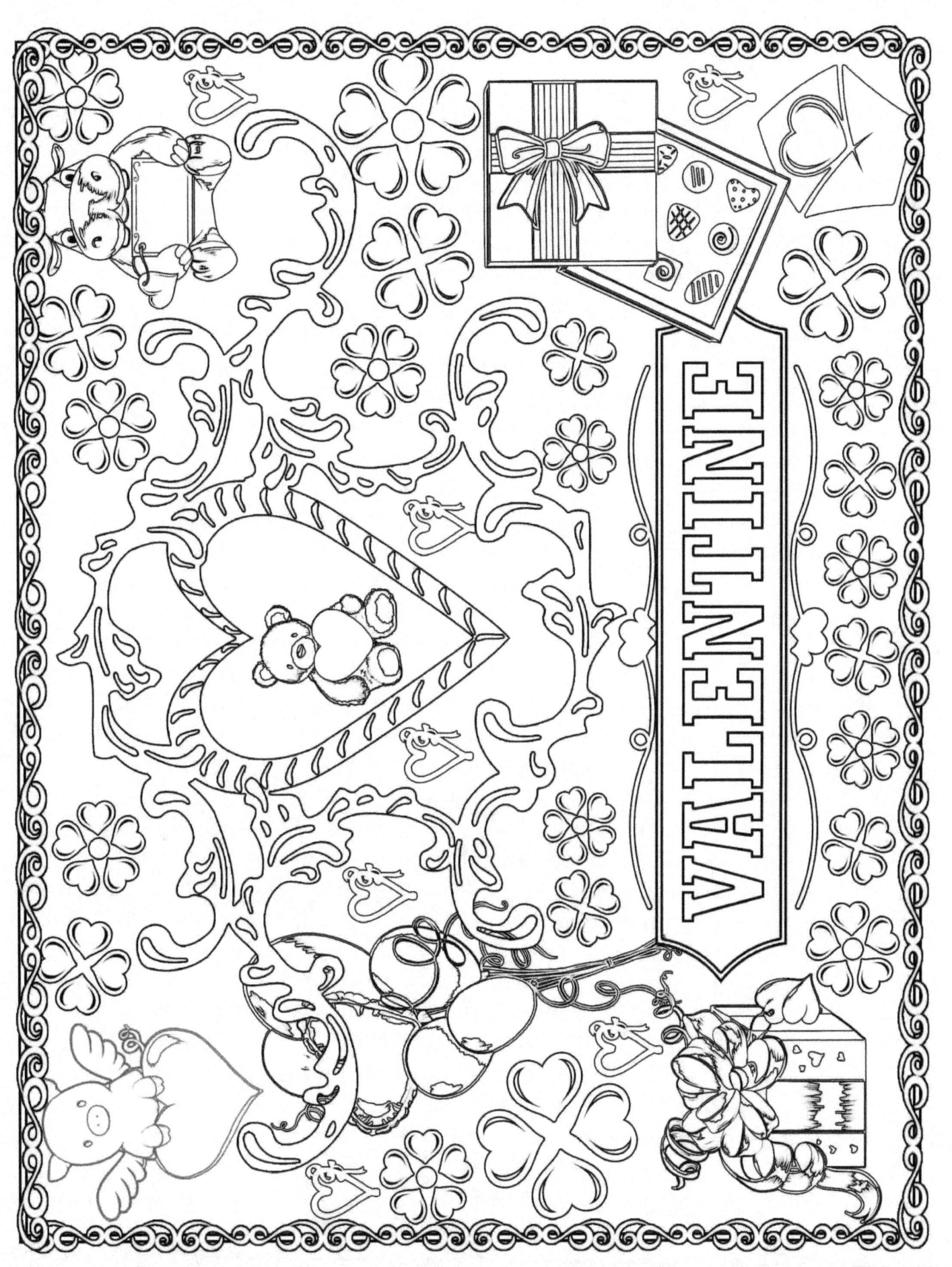

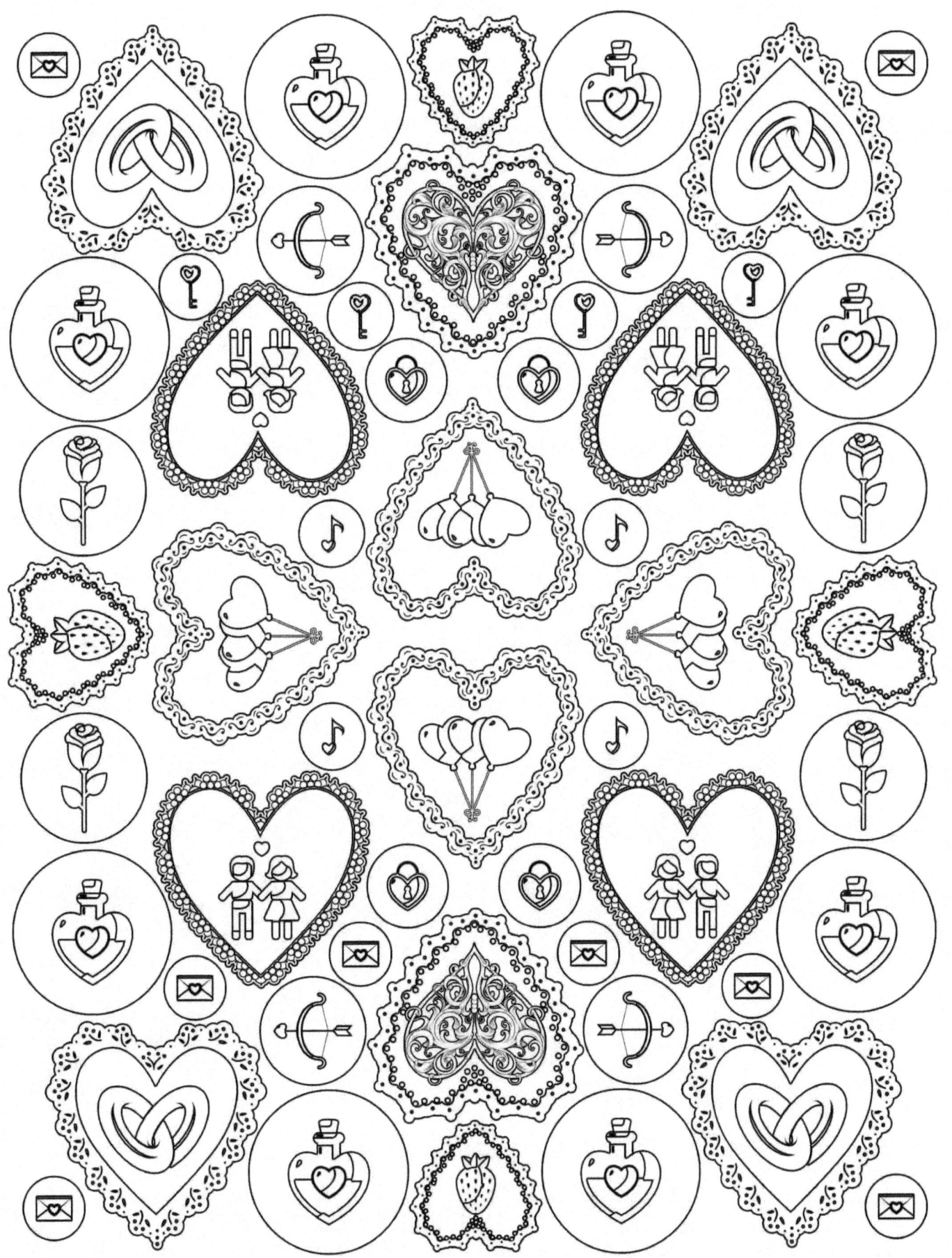

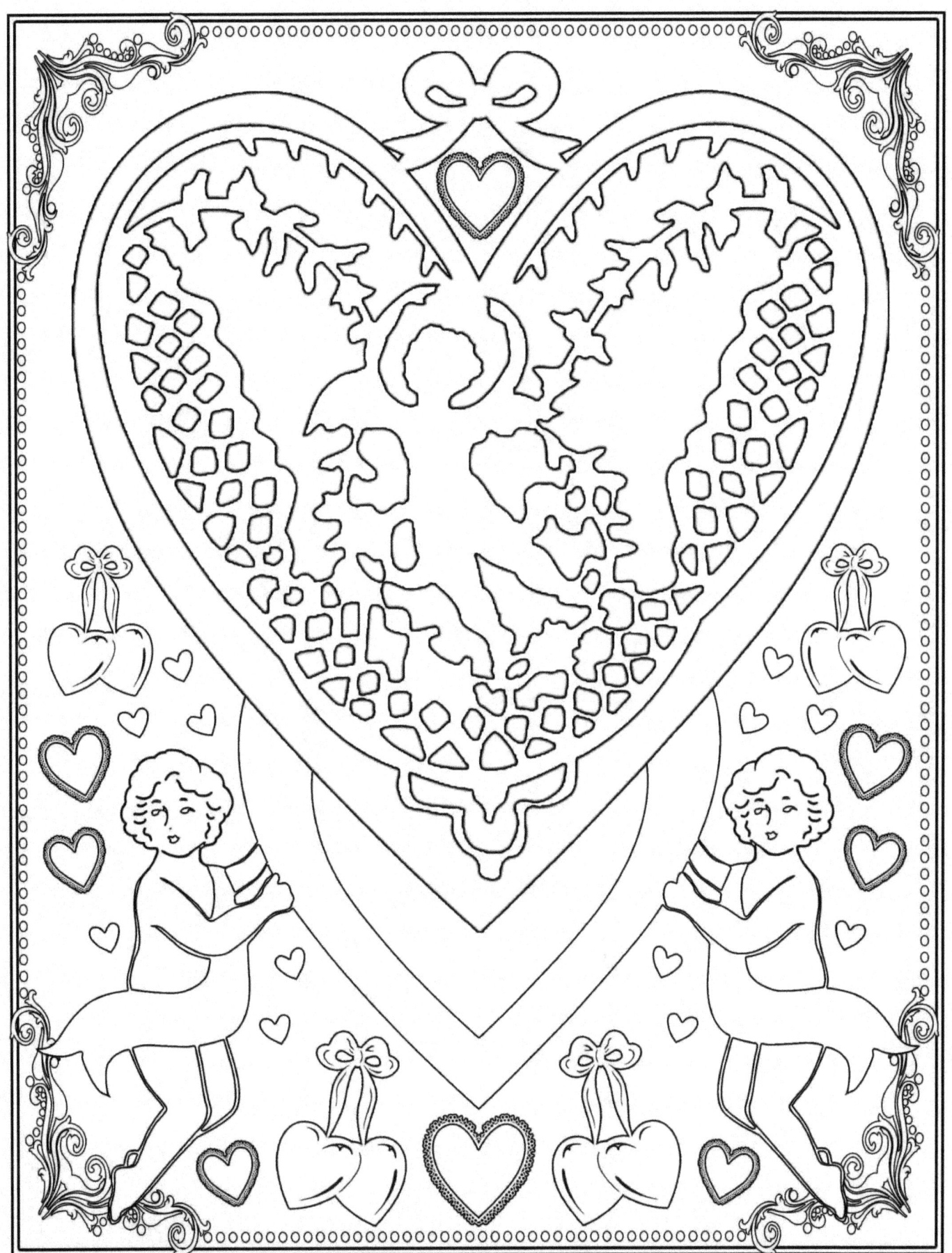

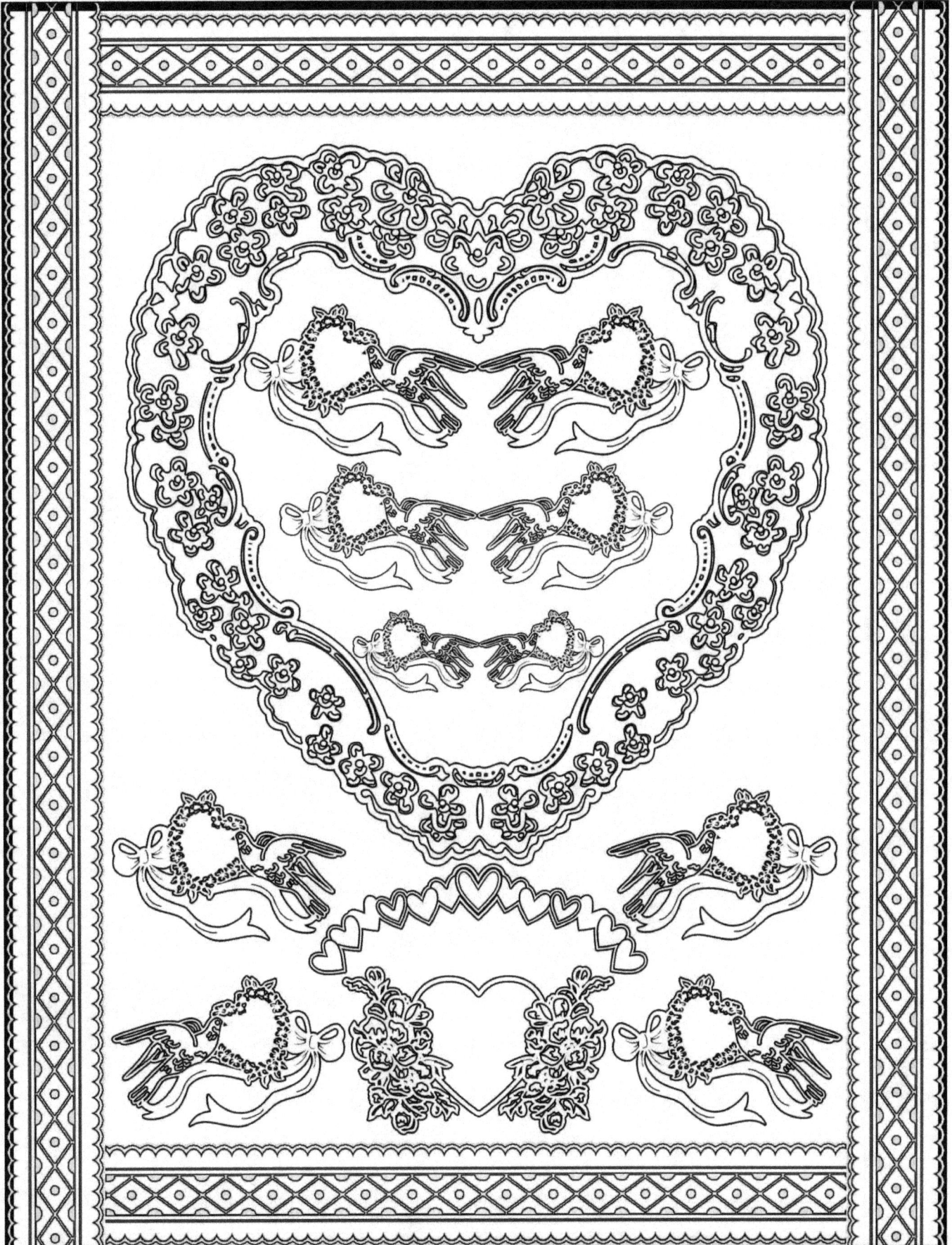

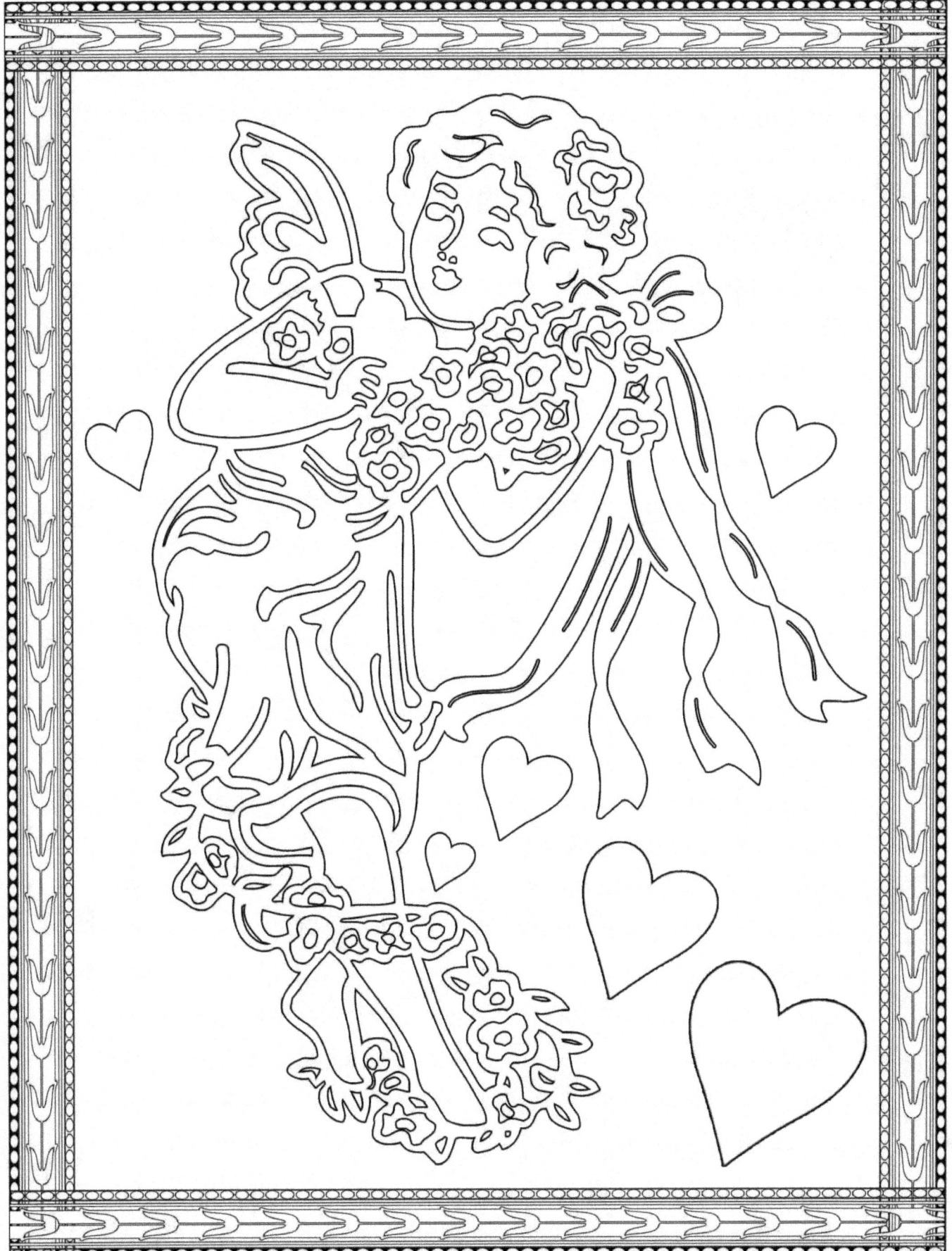

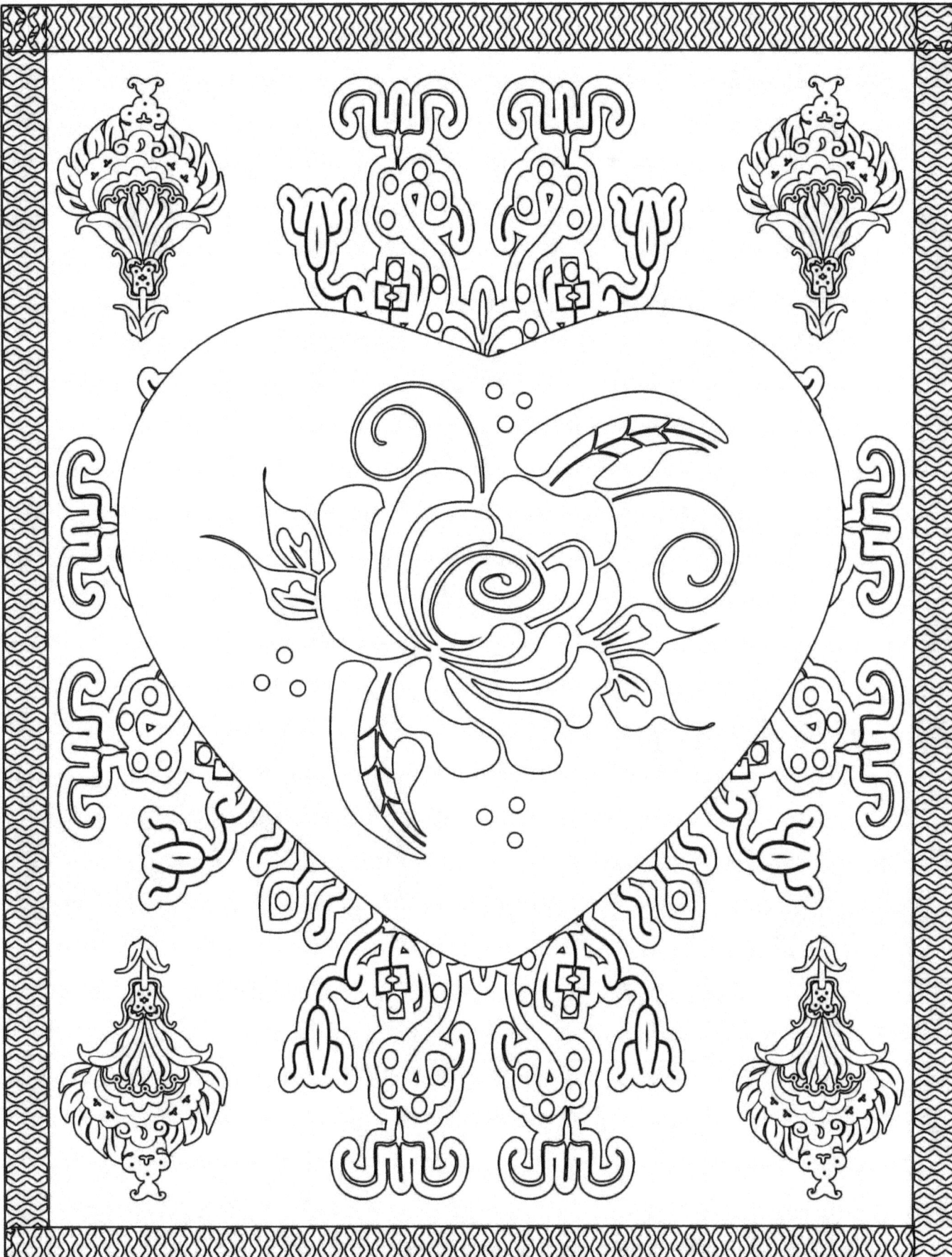

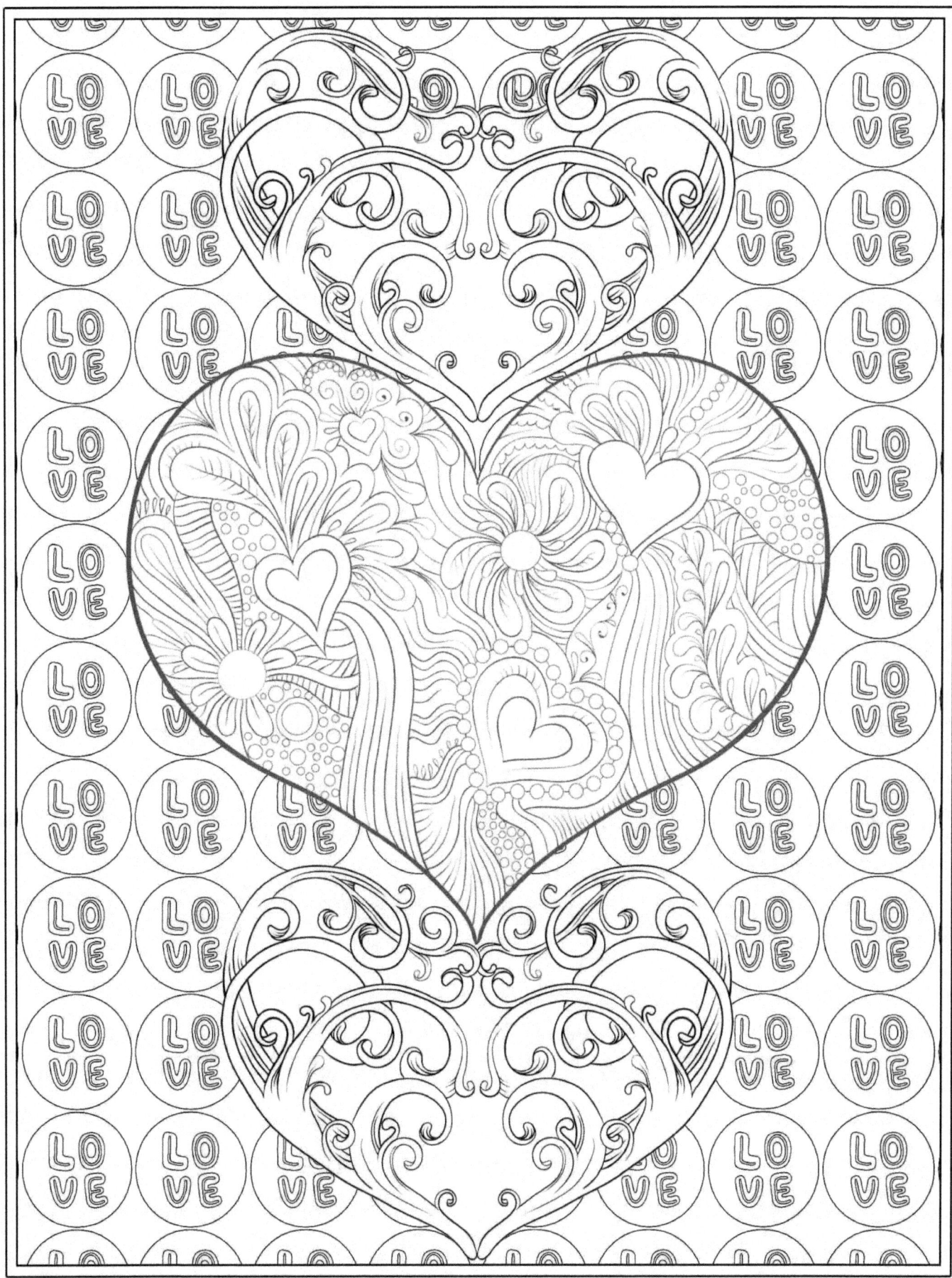

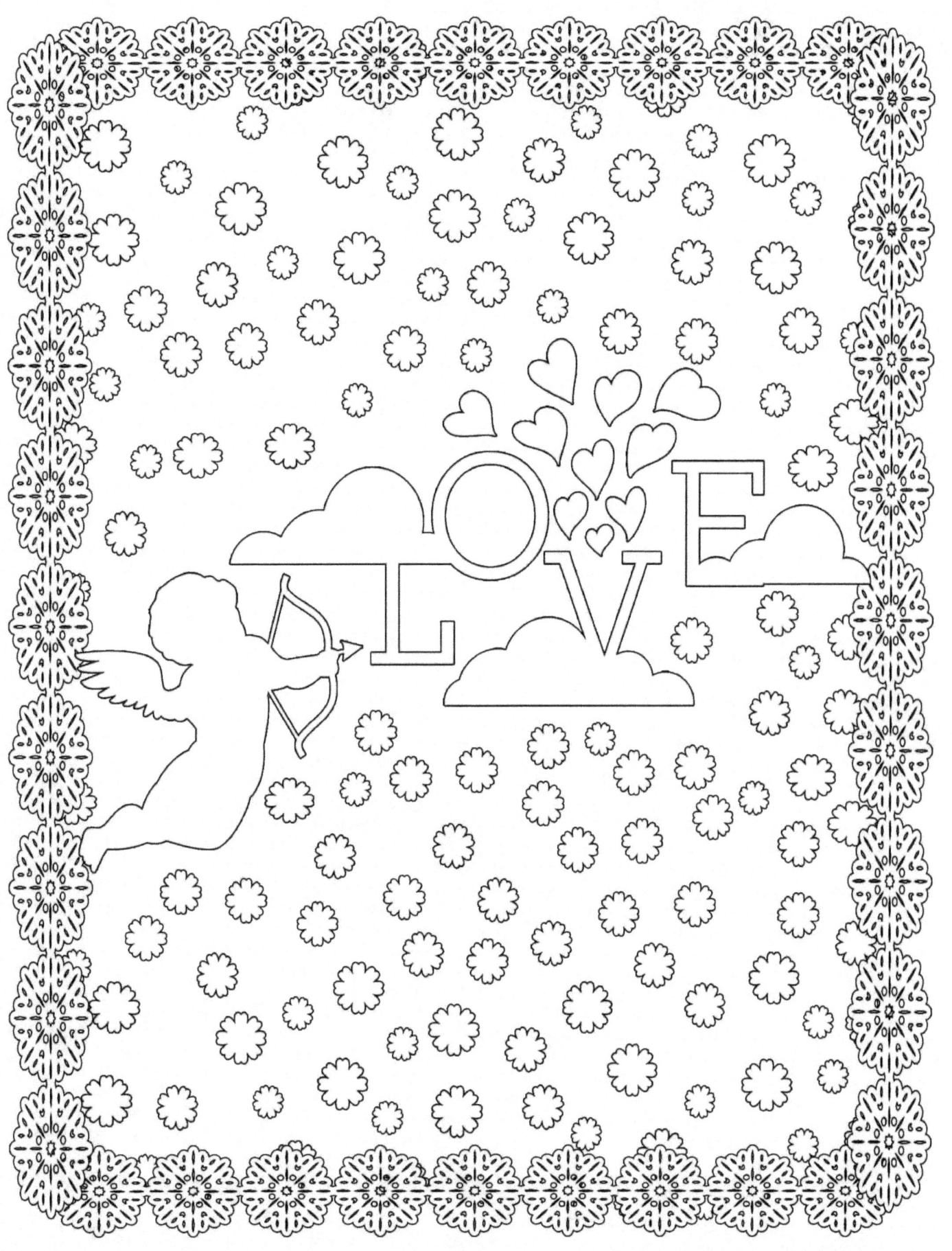

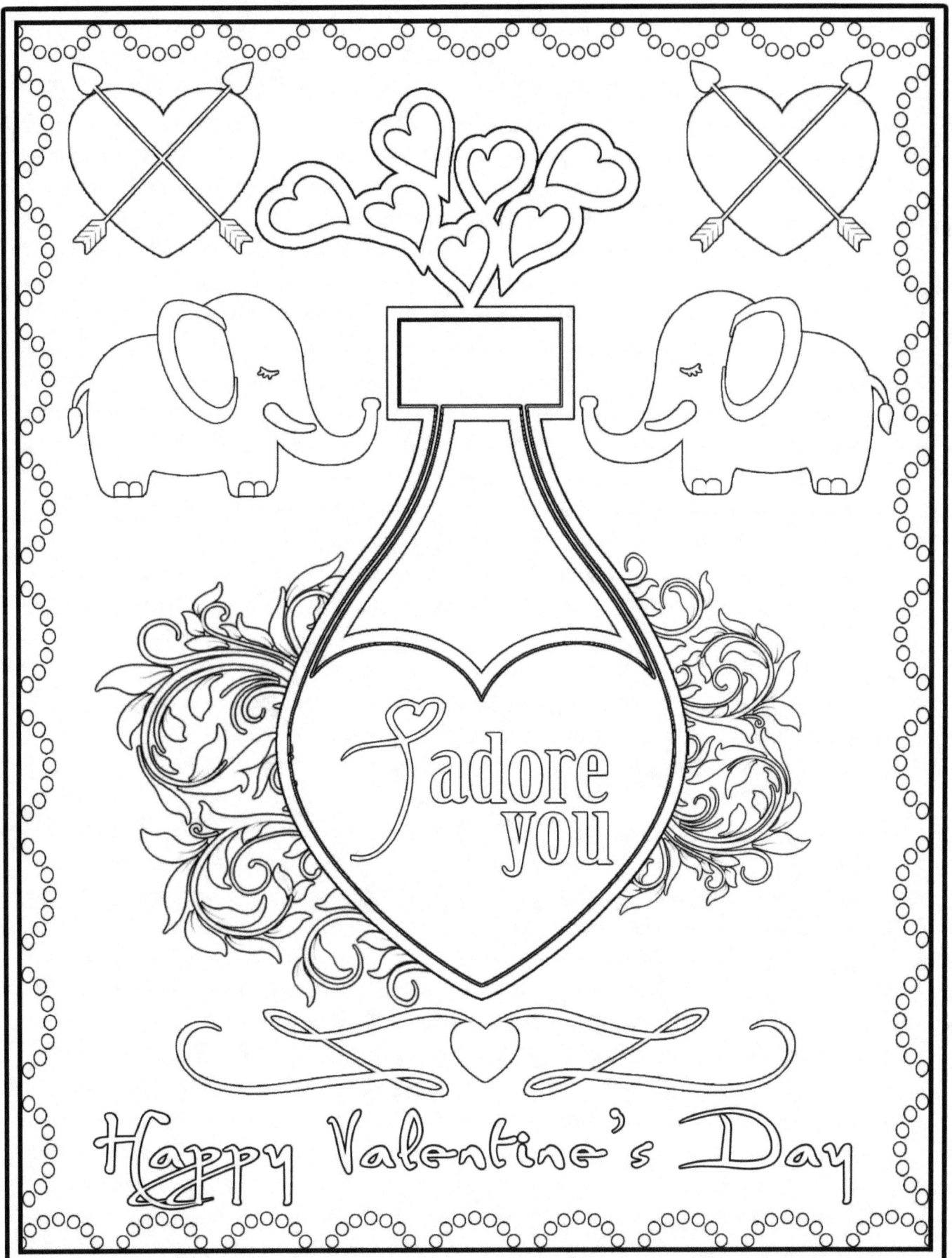

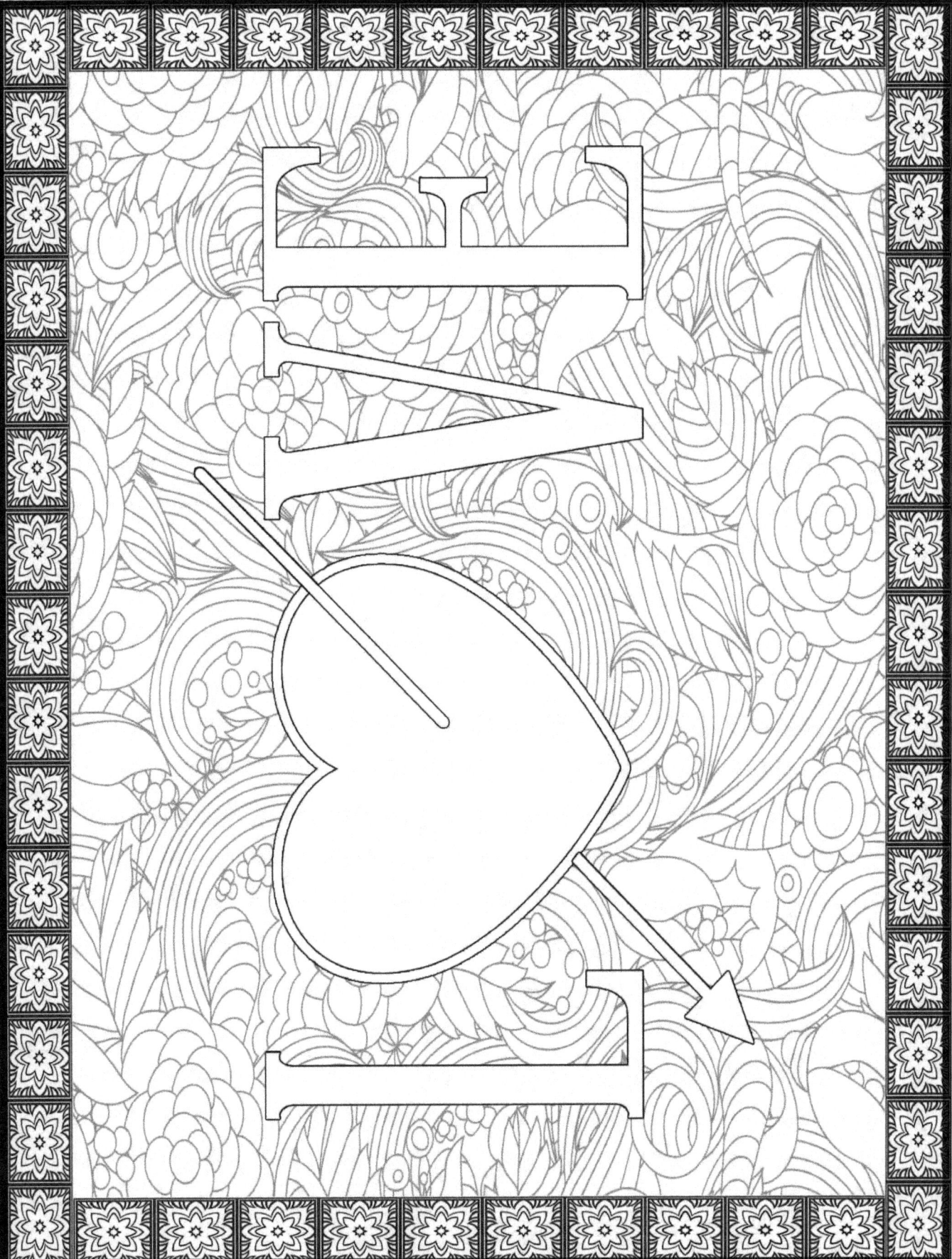

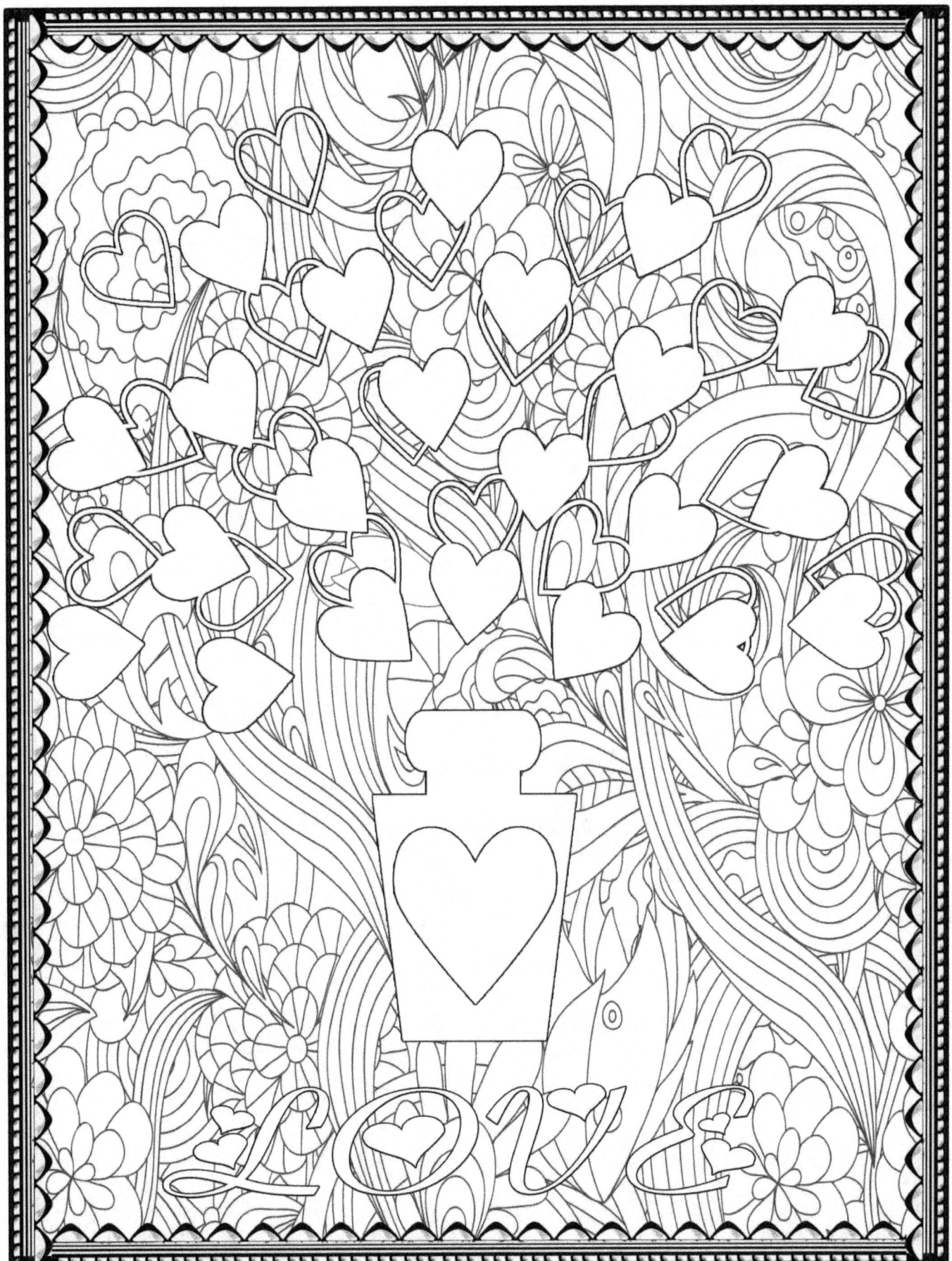

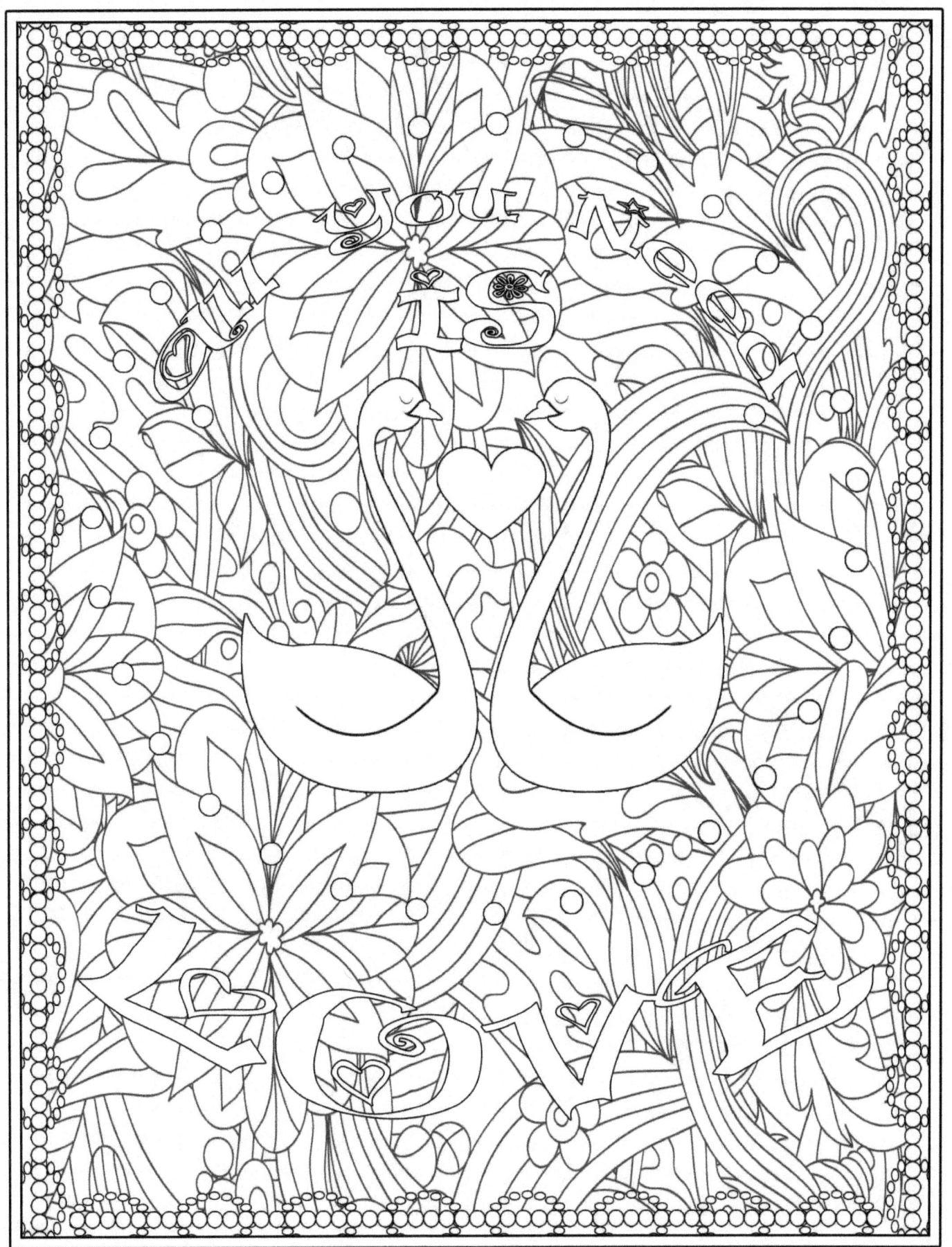

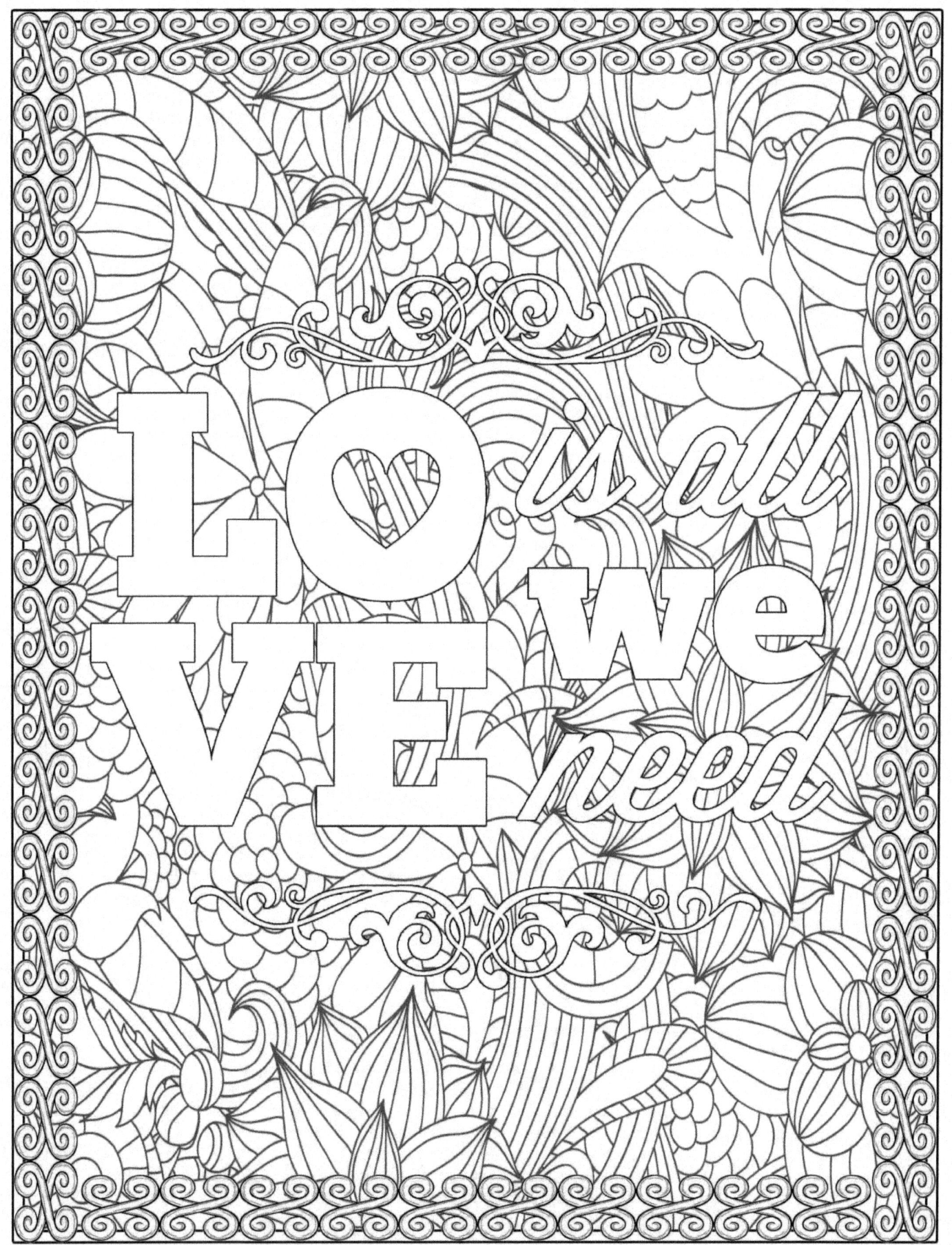

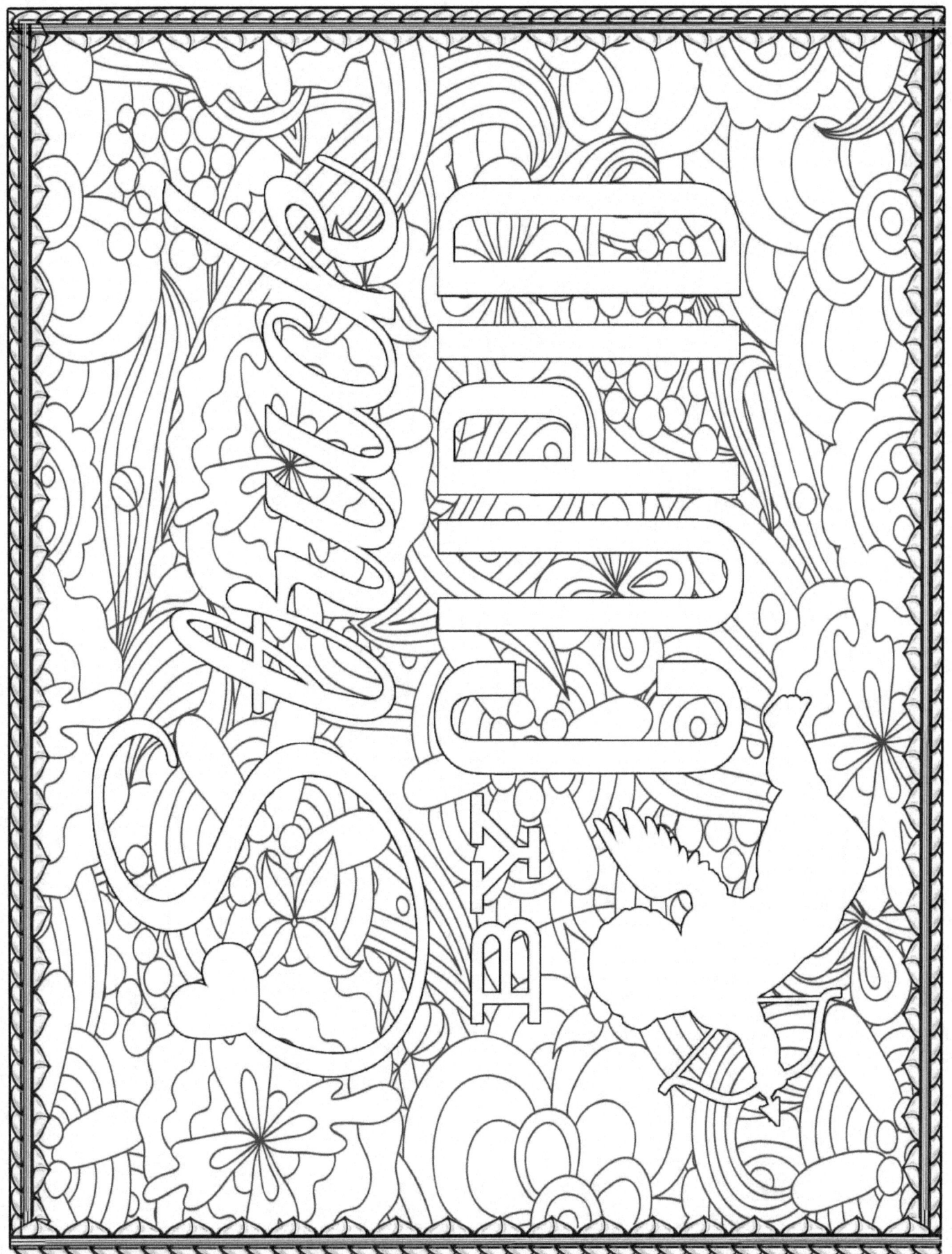

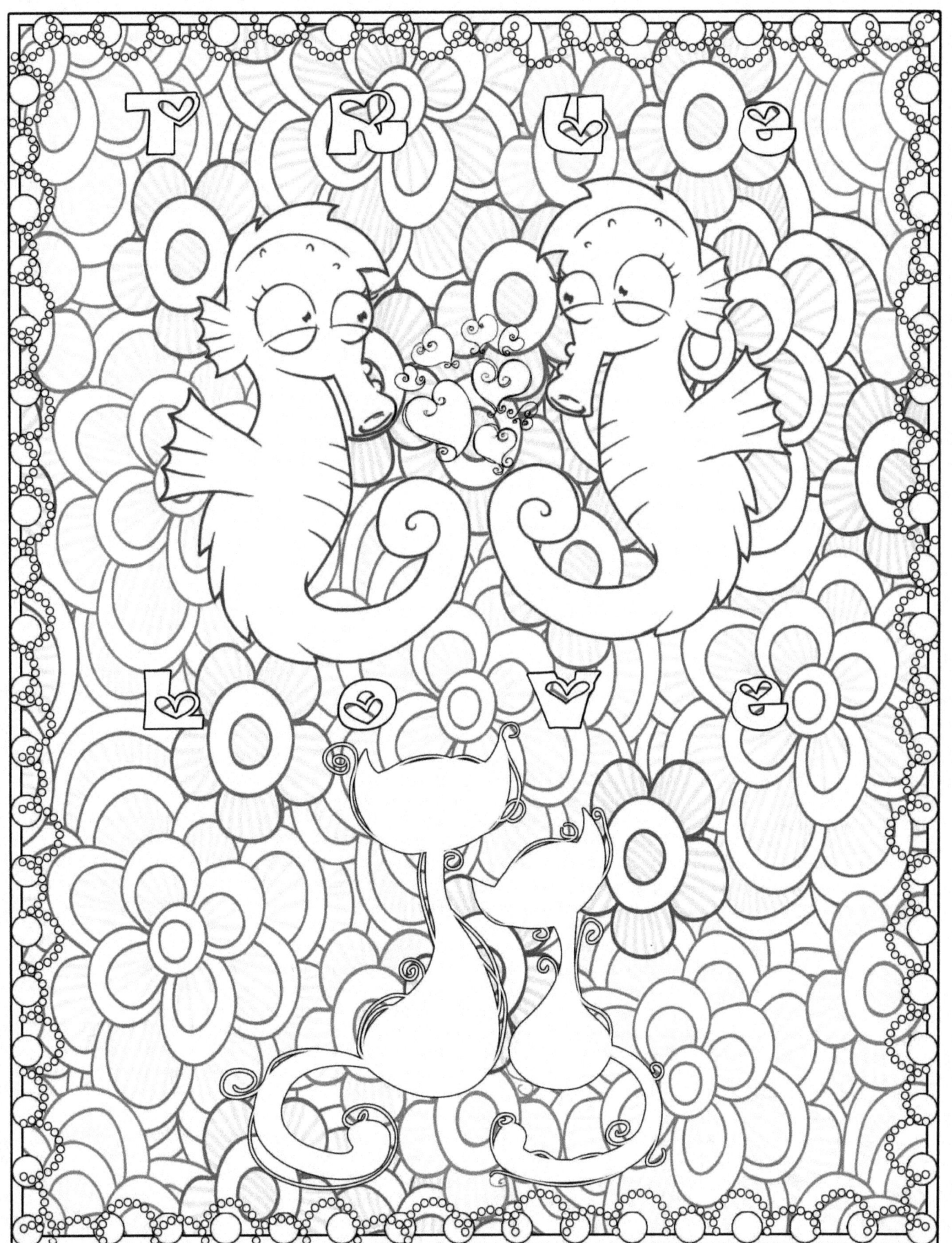

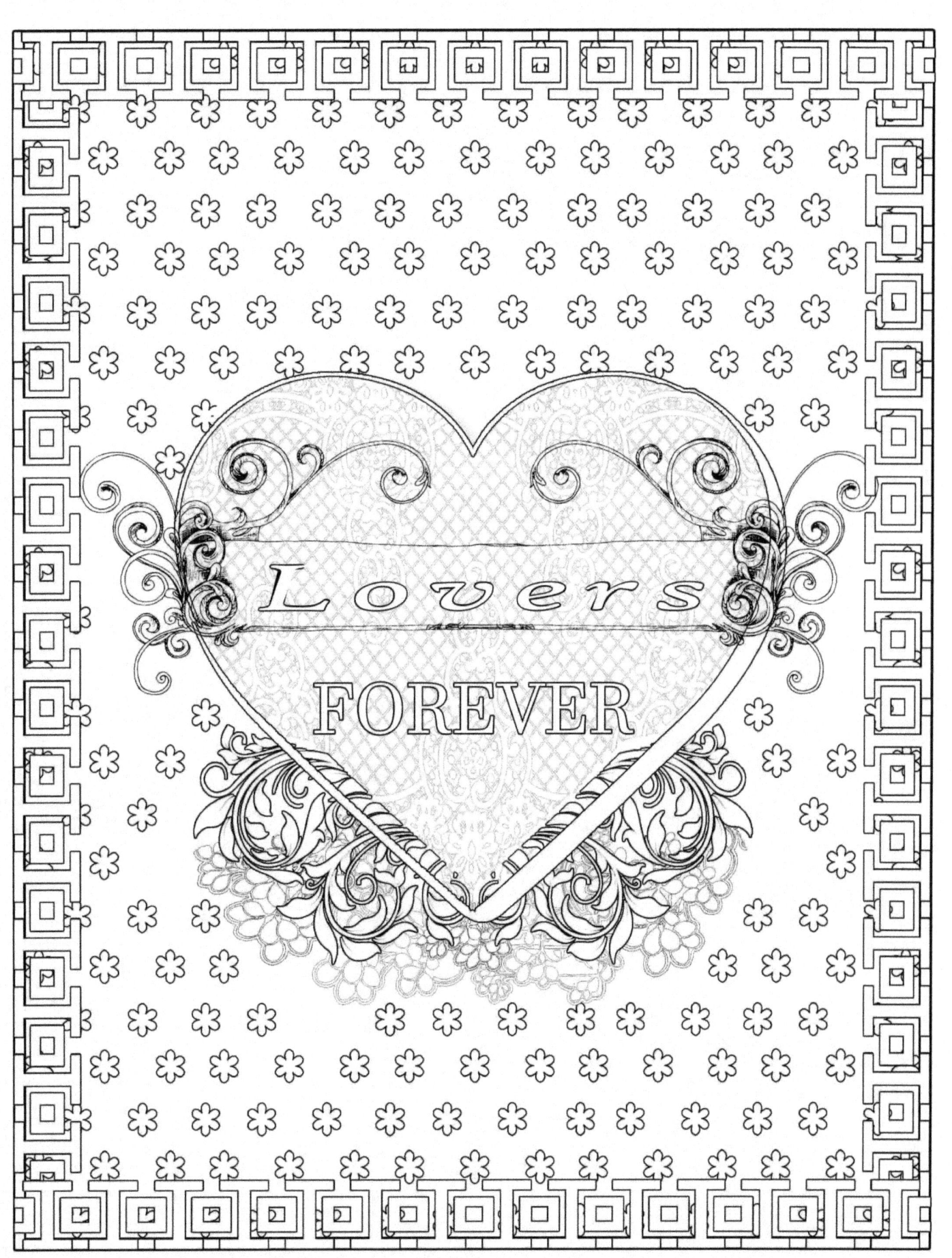

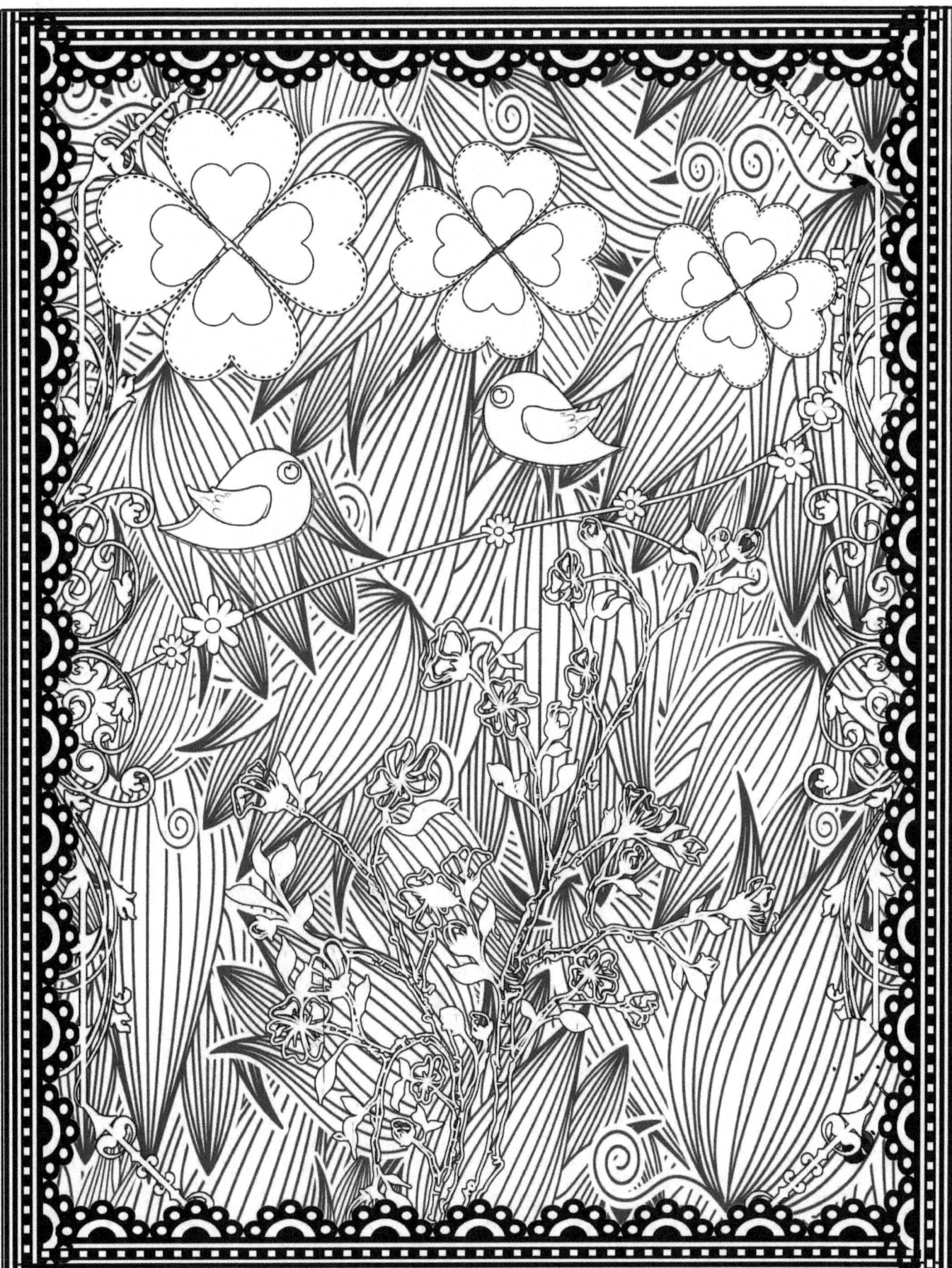

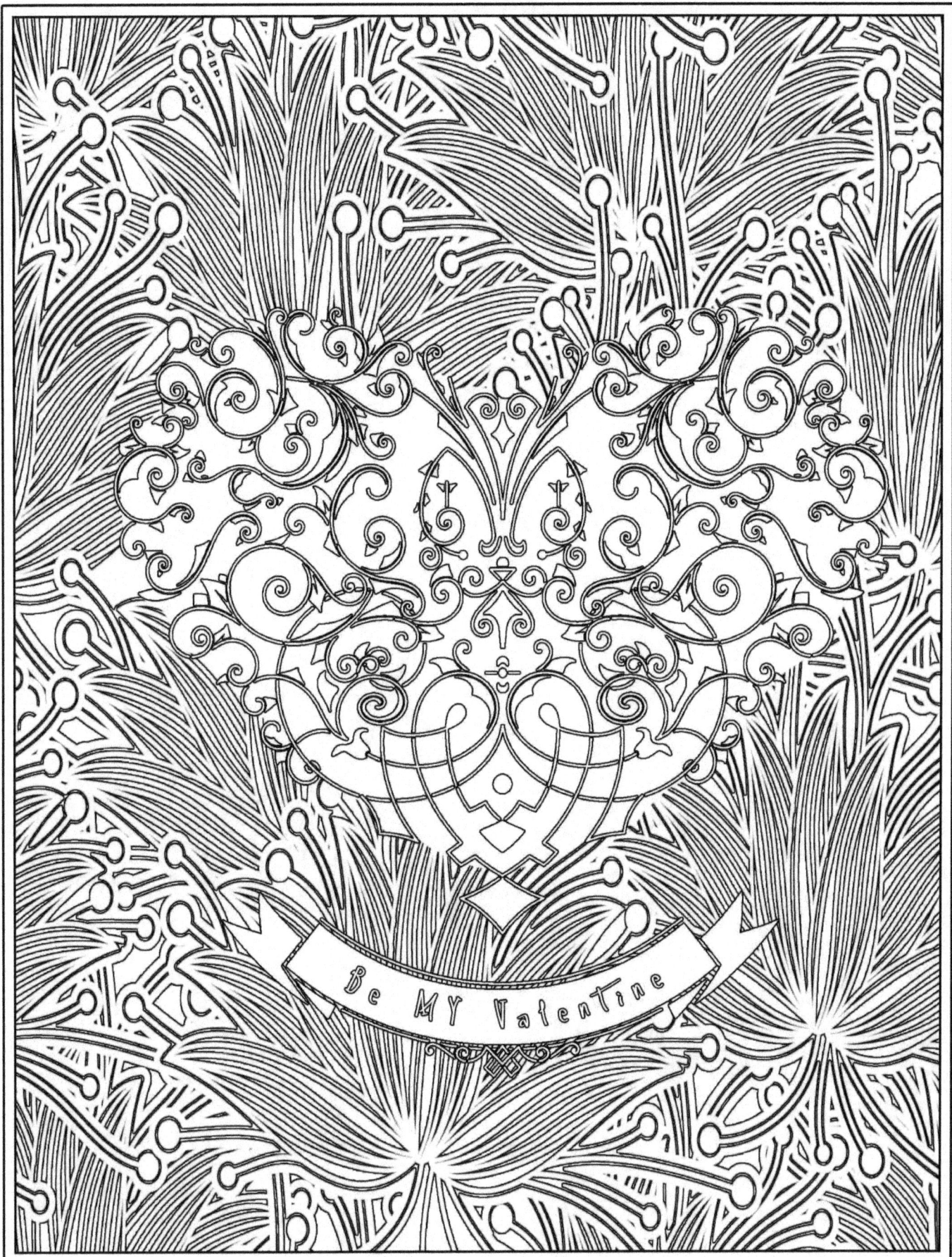

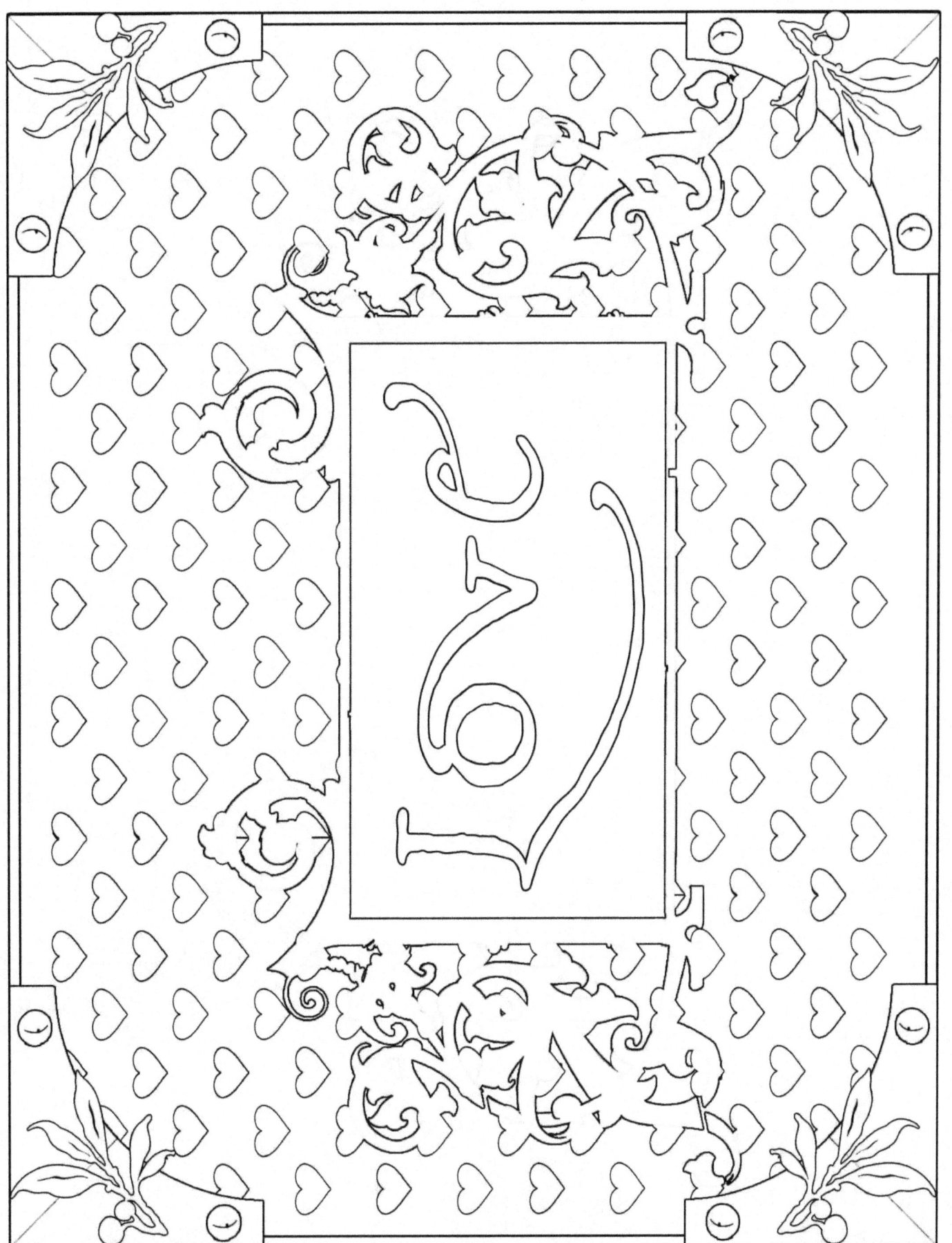

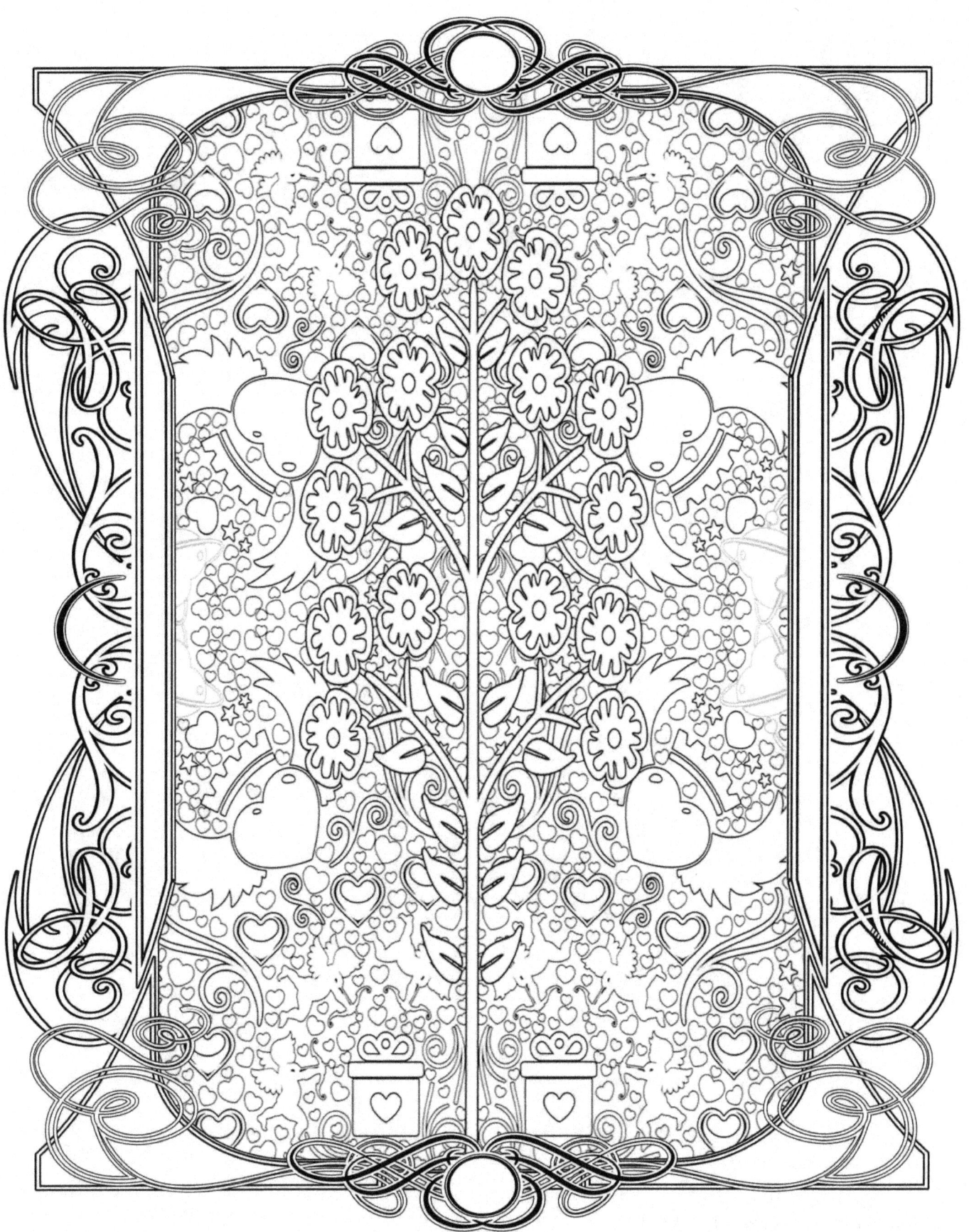

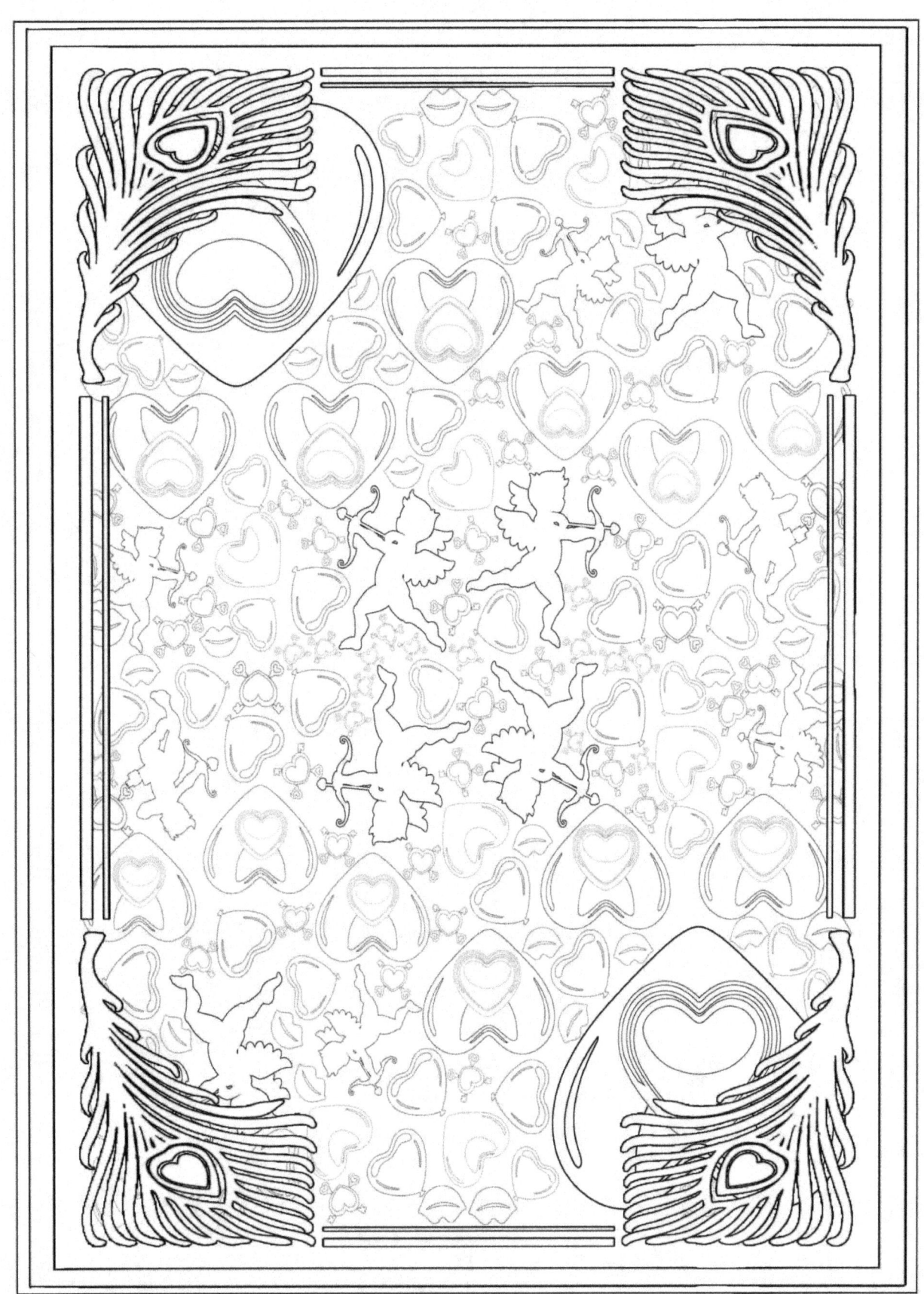

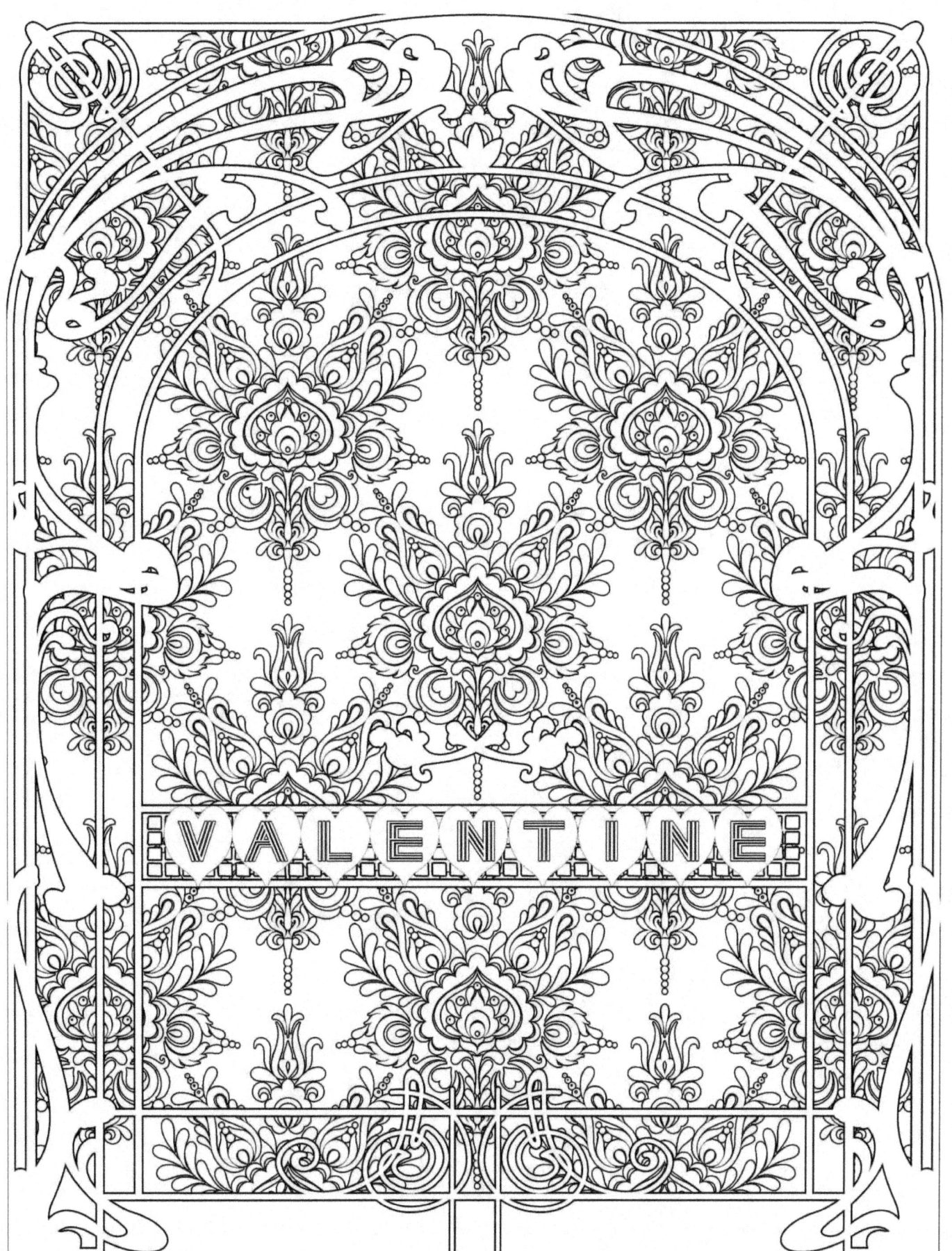

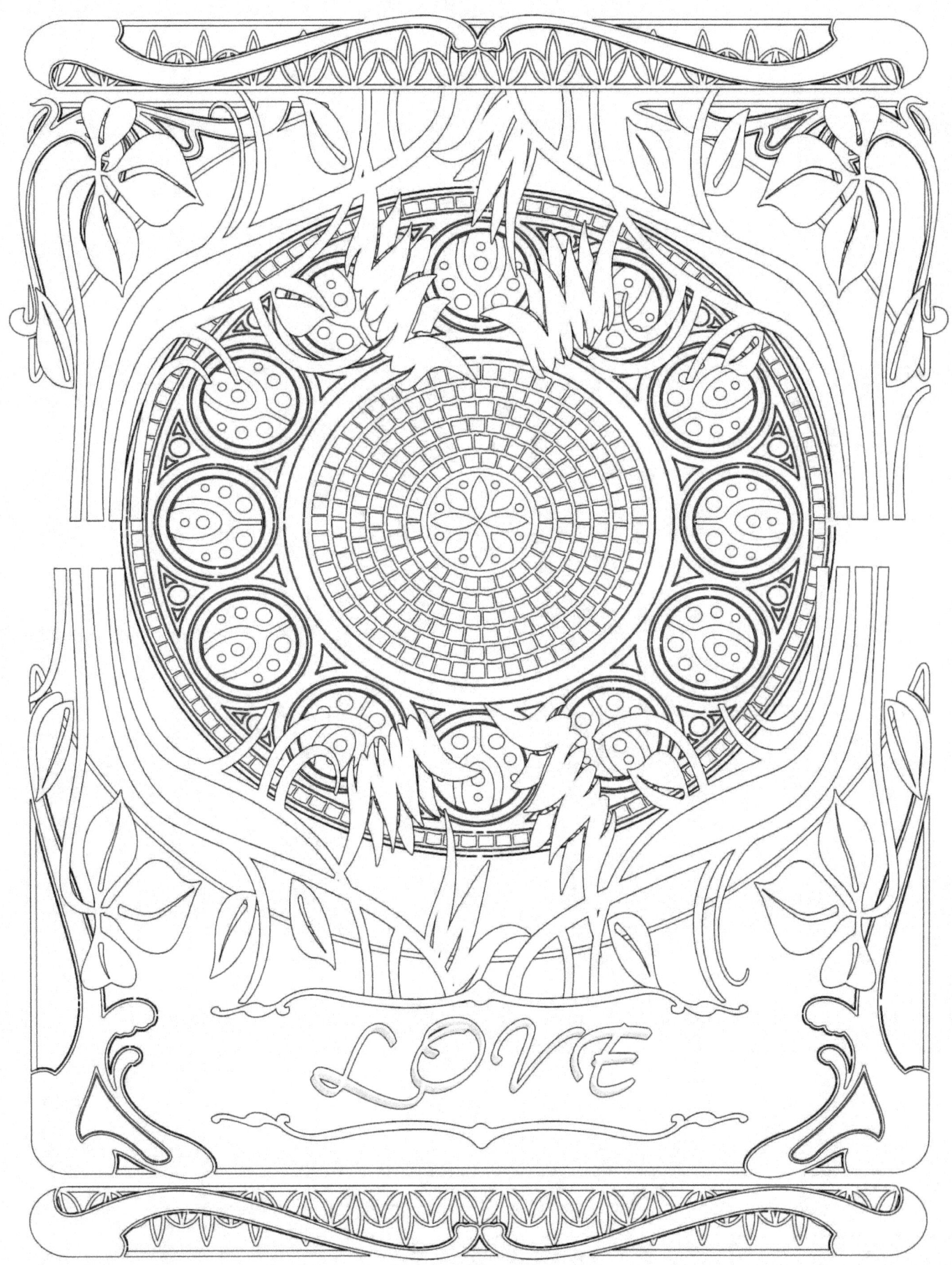

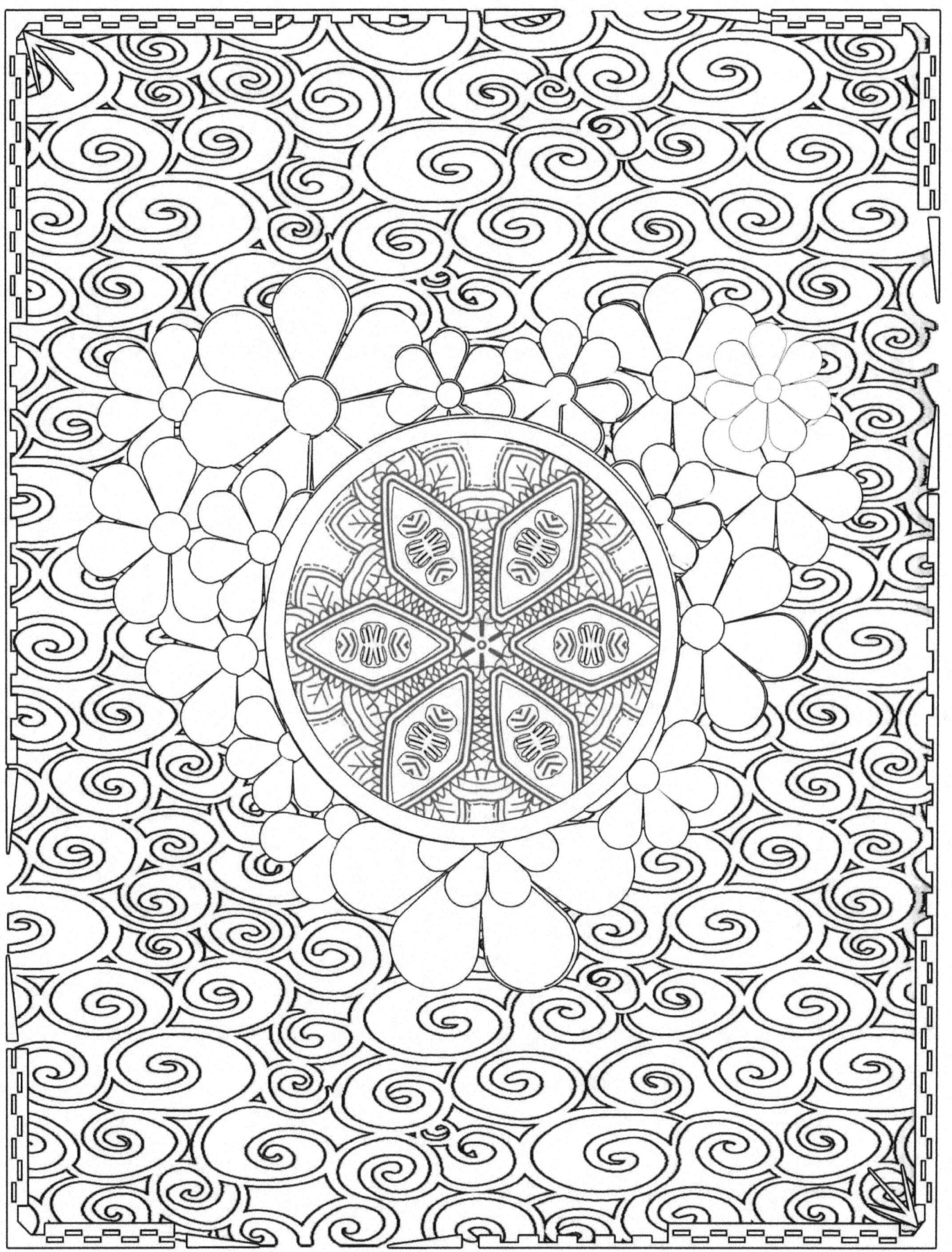

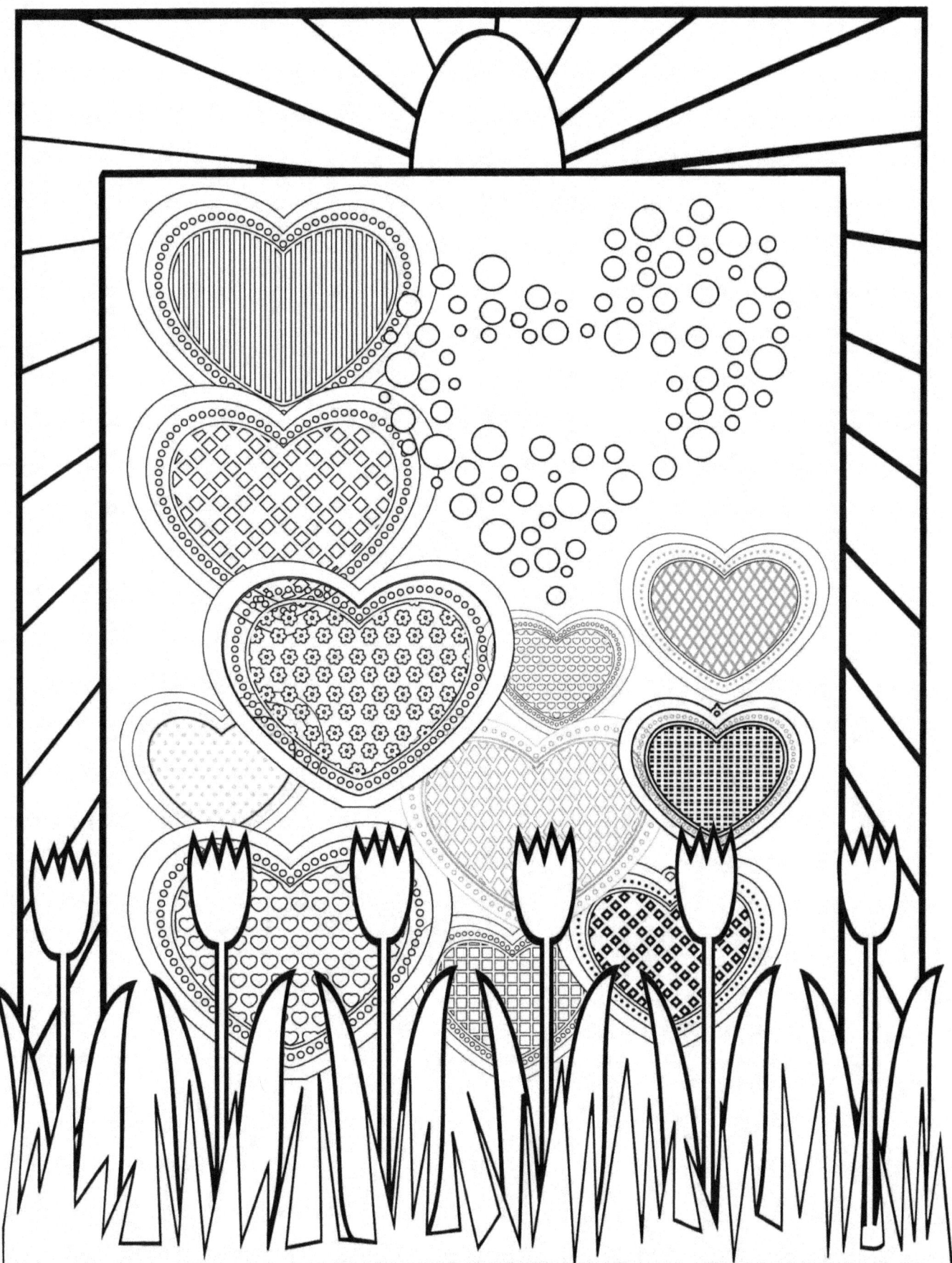

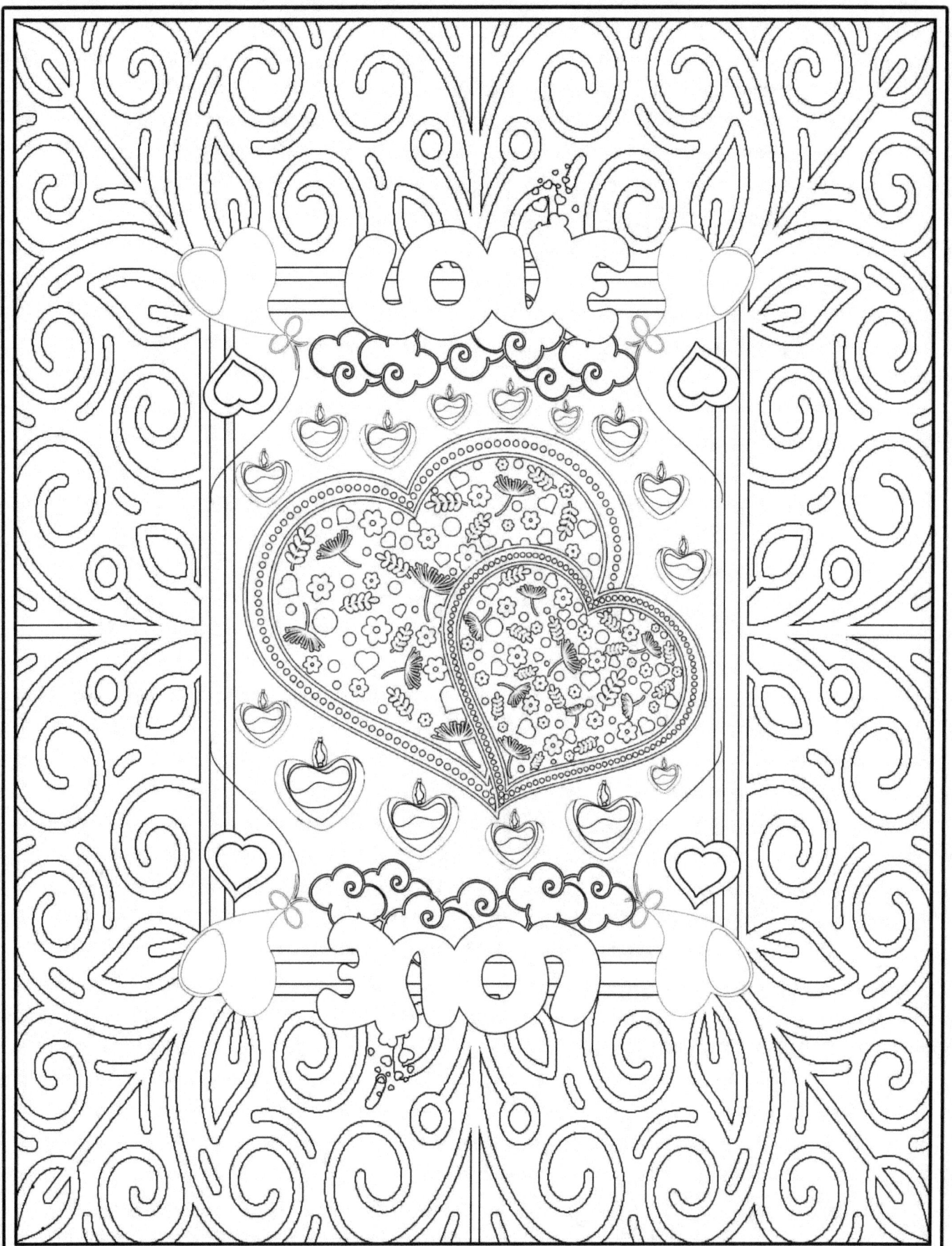

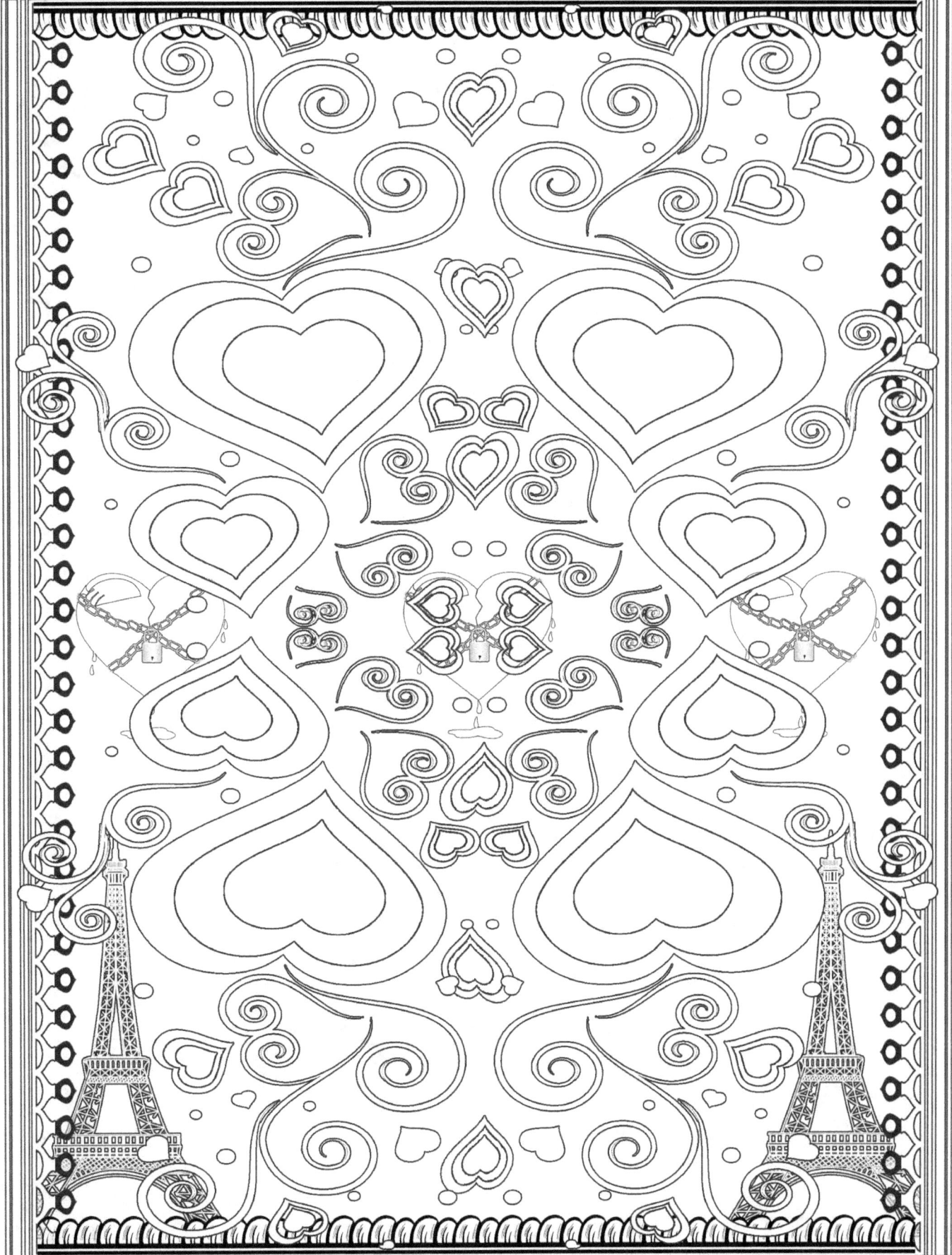

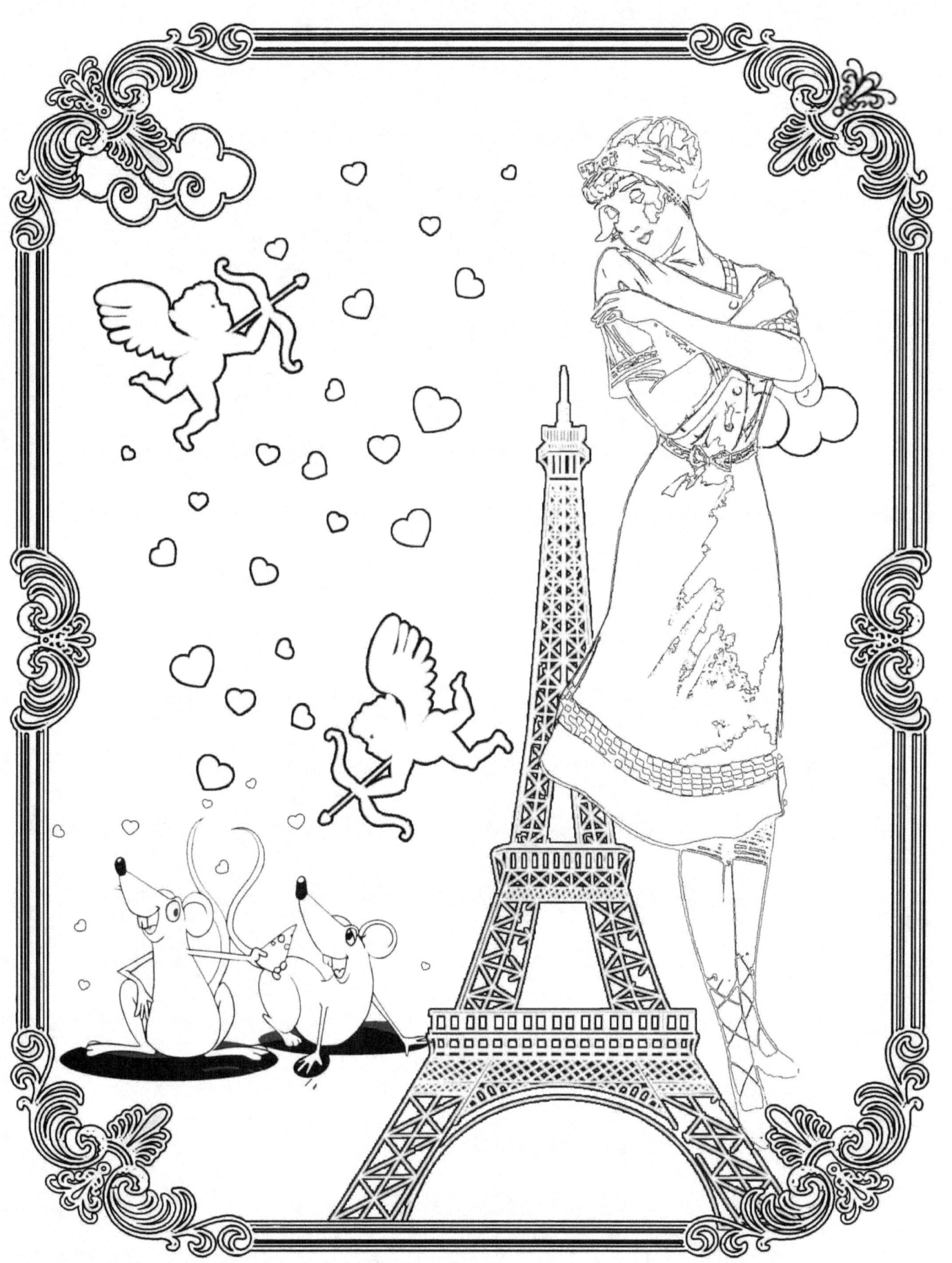

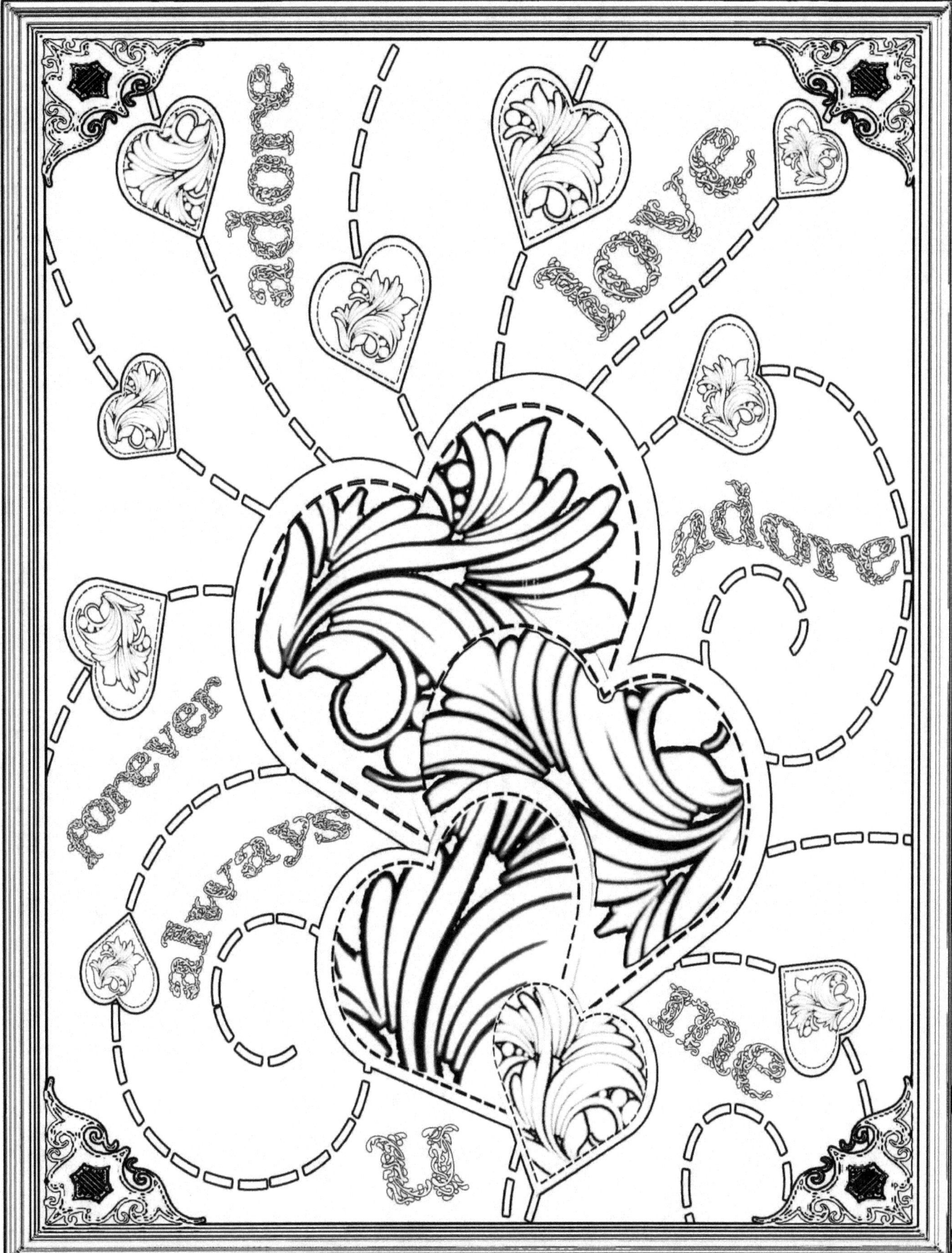

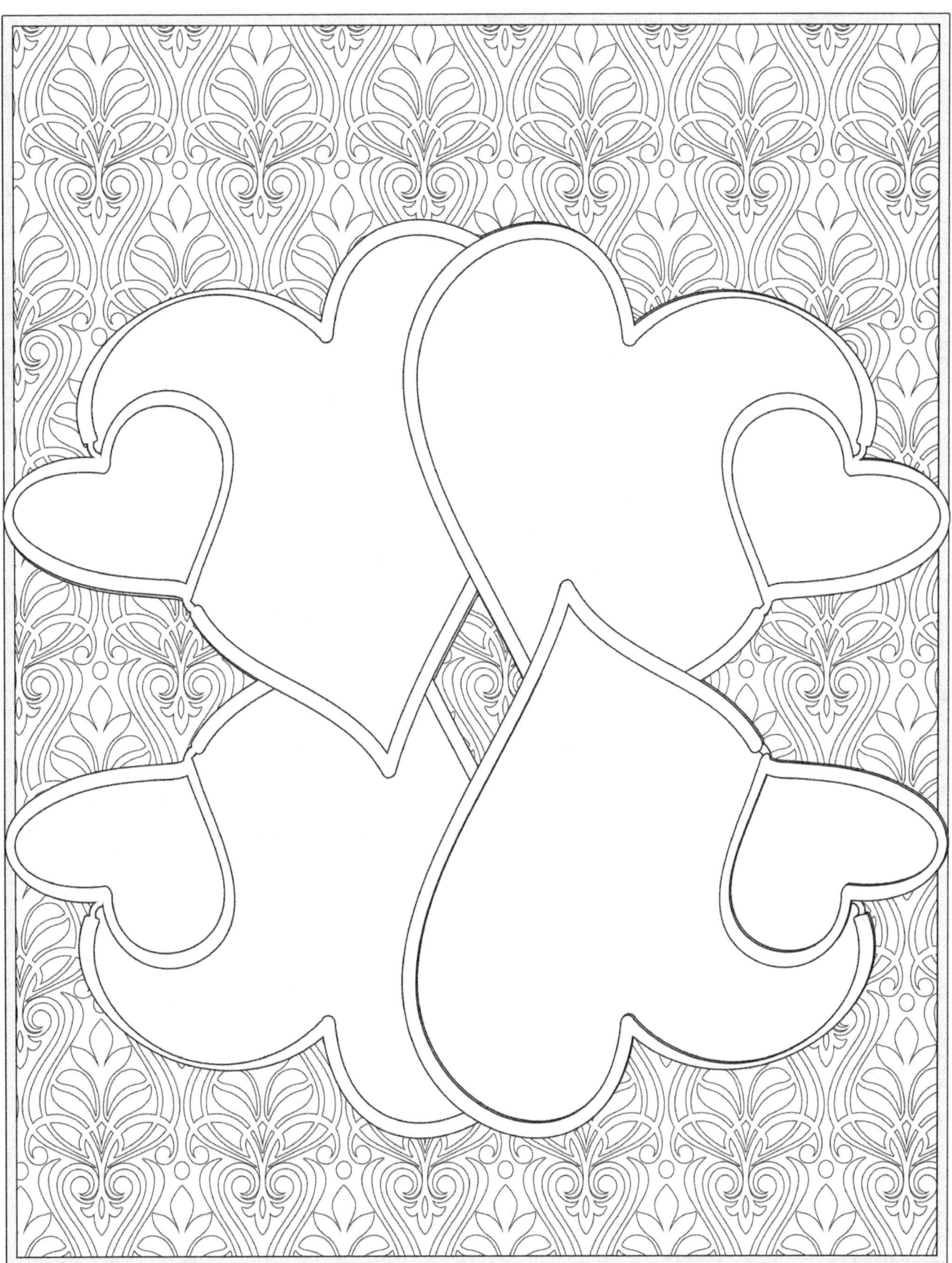

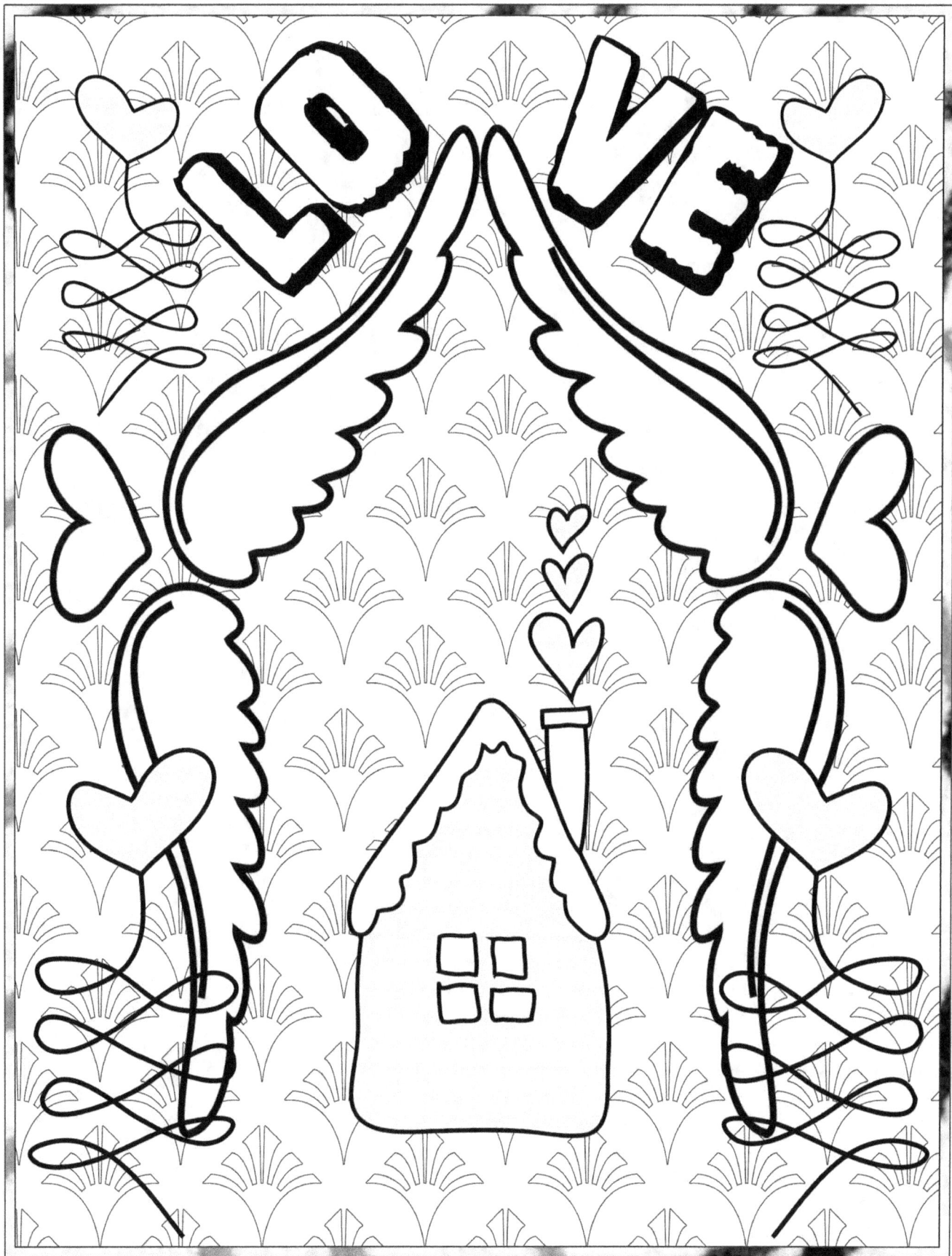

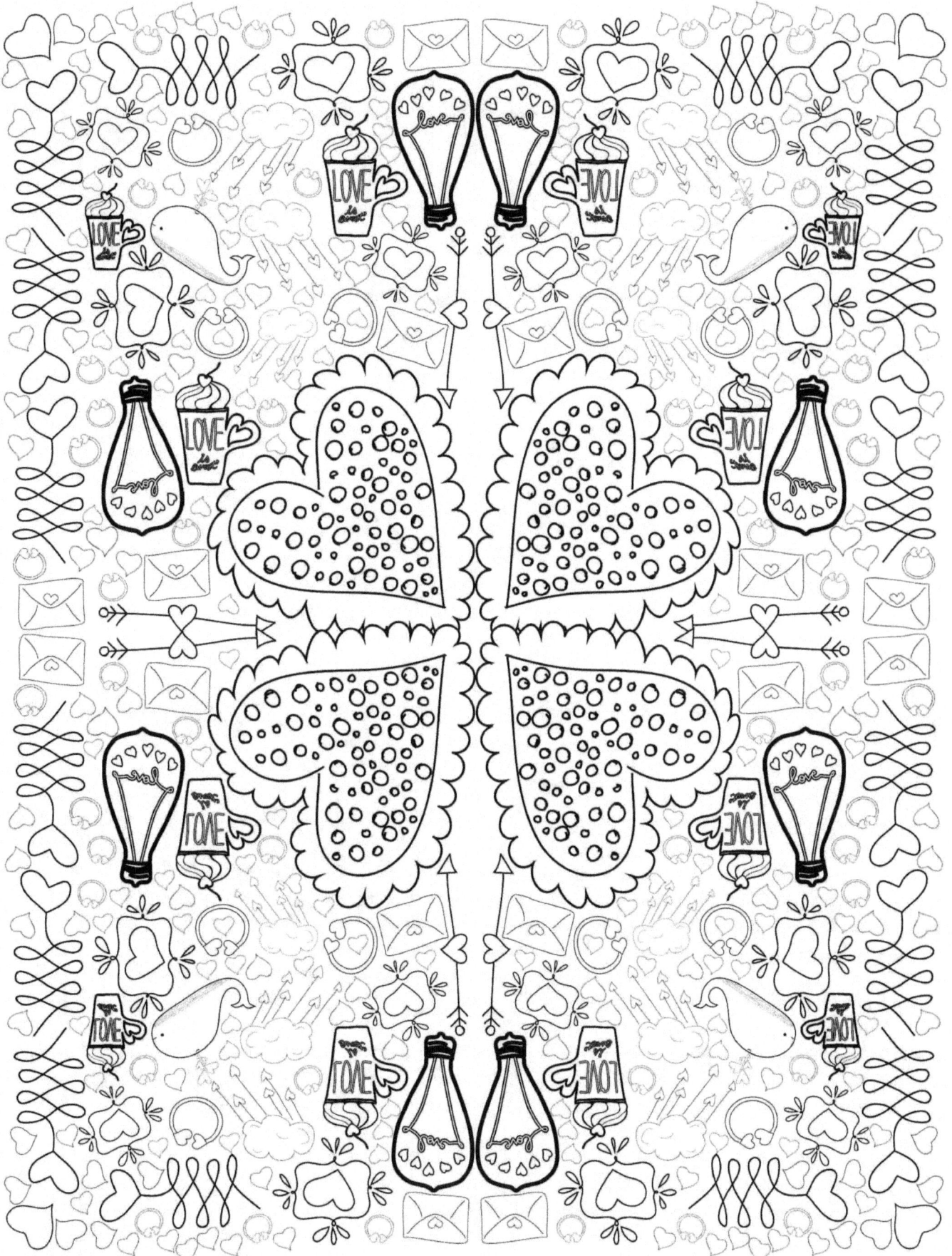

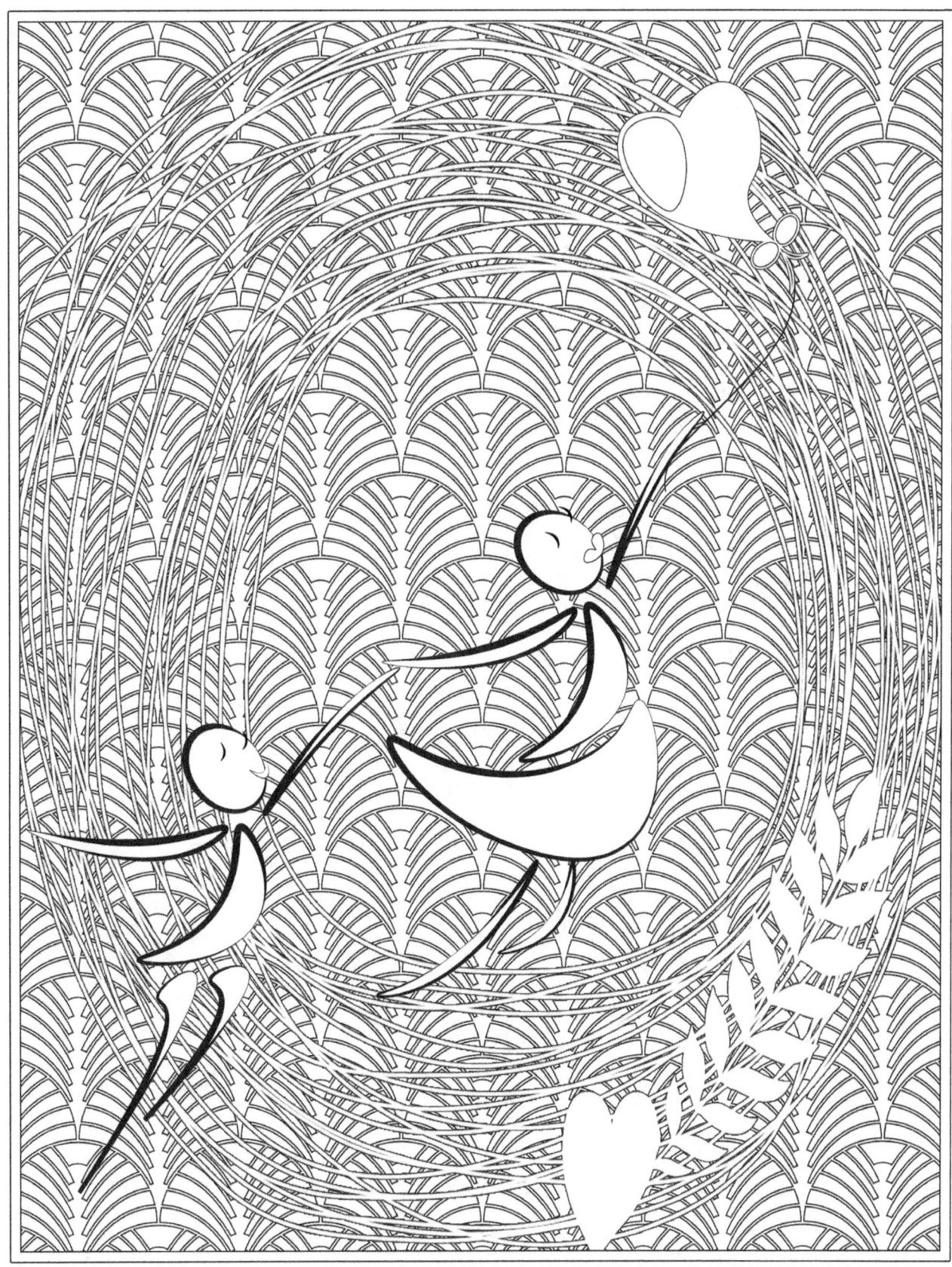

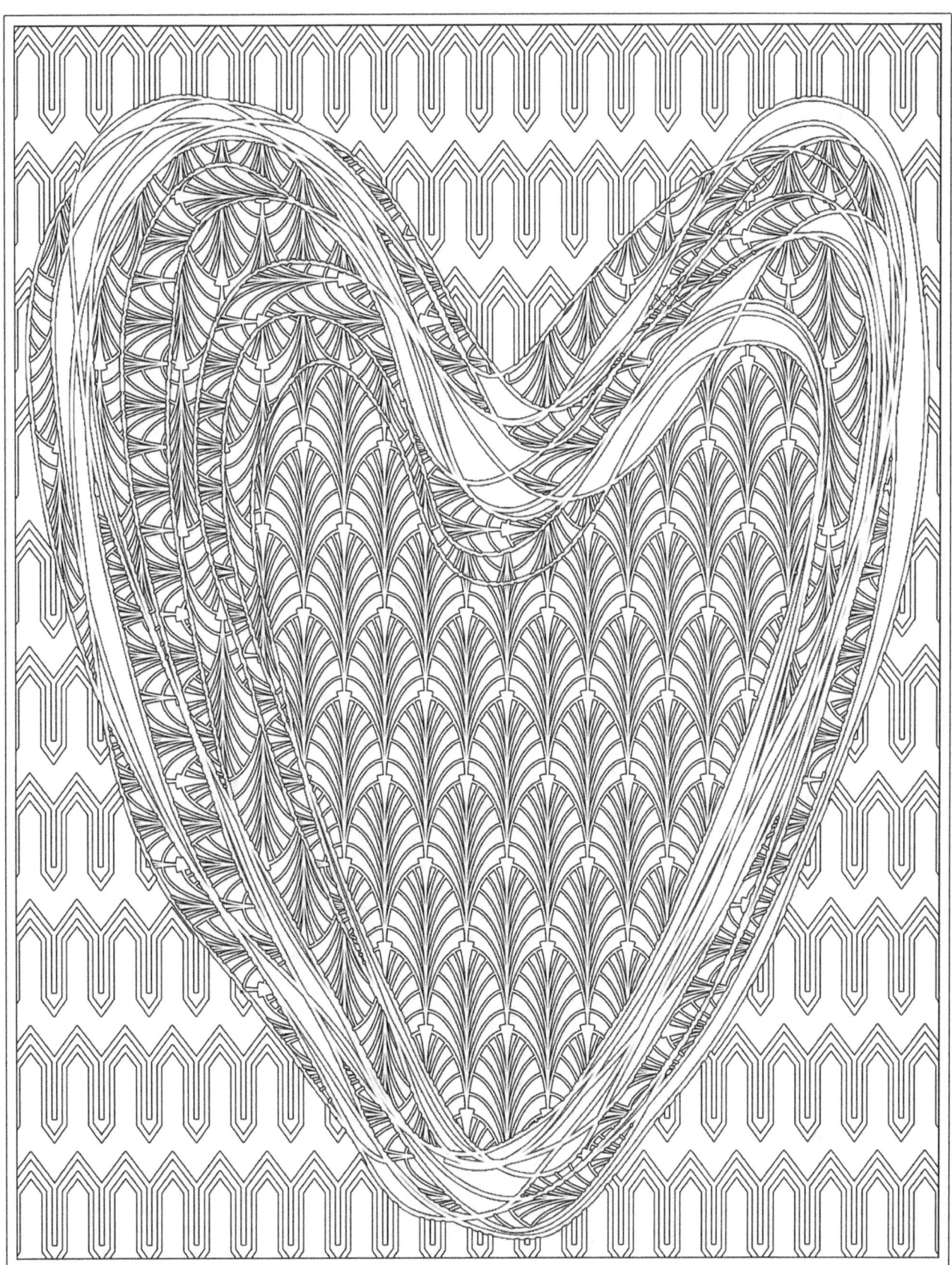

kisses

hugs

truelove

sweet

passion   kind

be loved

romance   cupid   birds   joy

sweetheart   kind   love

be mine   true

Valentine

always

forever

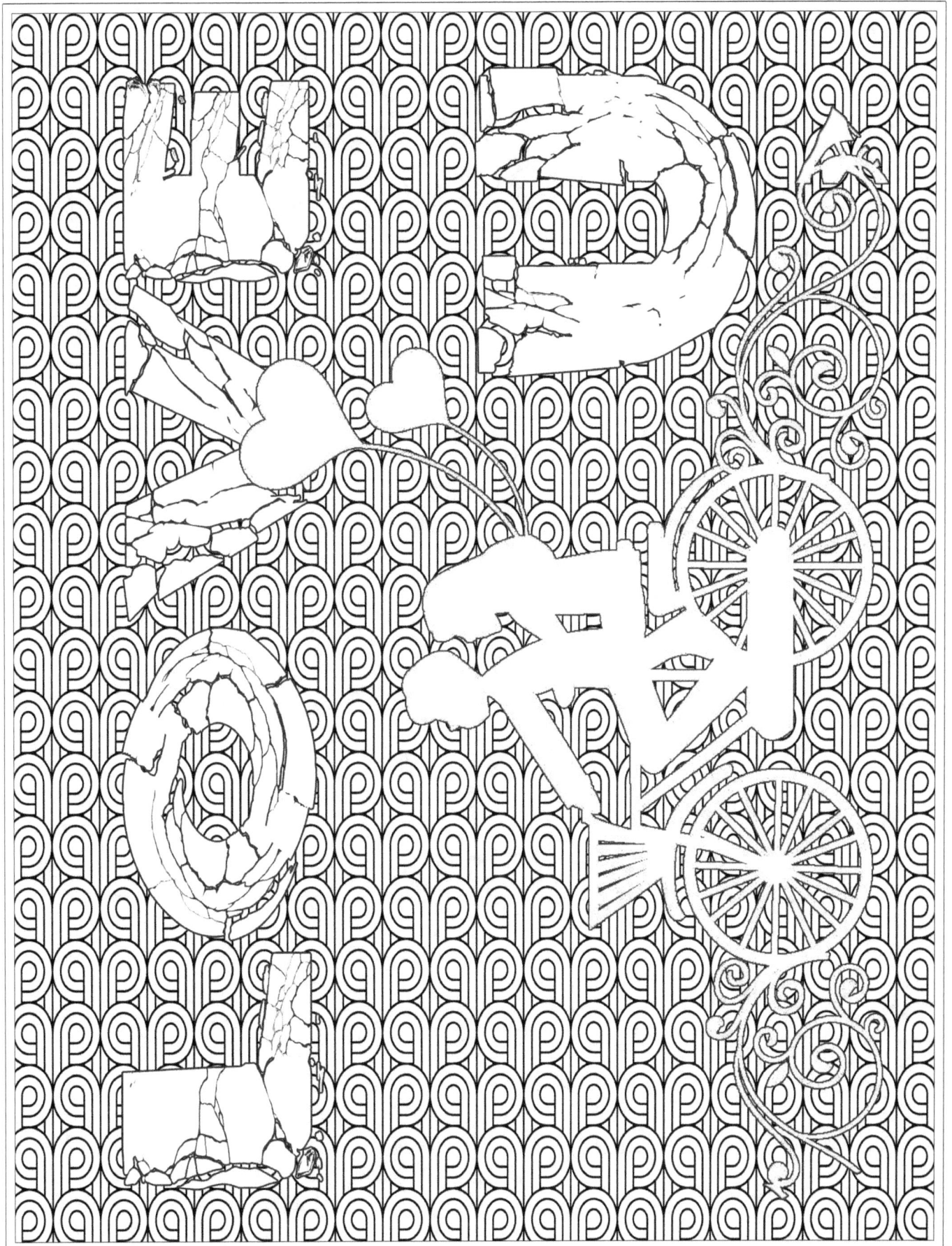

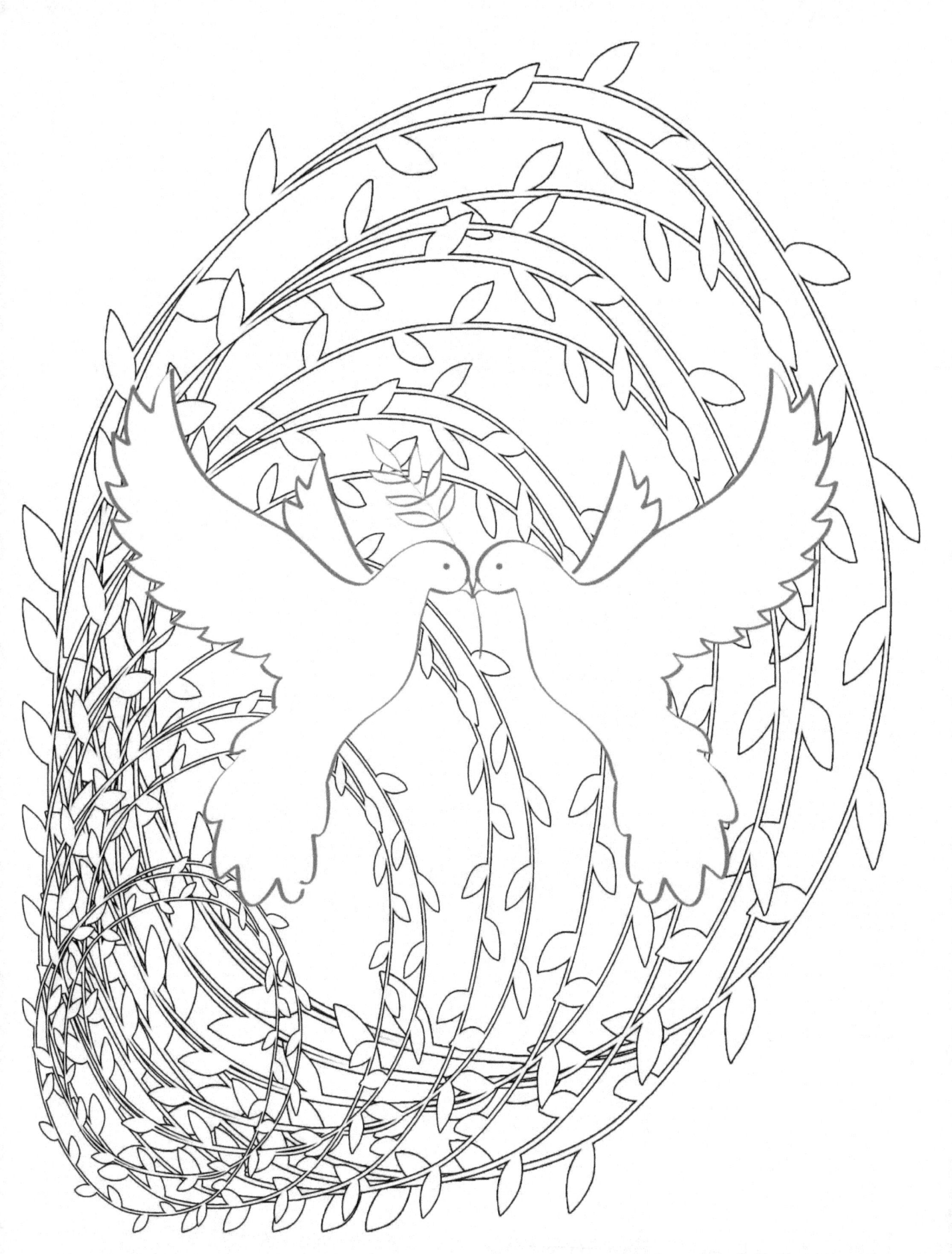

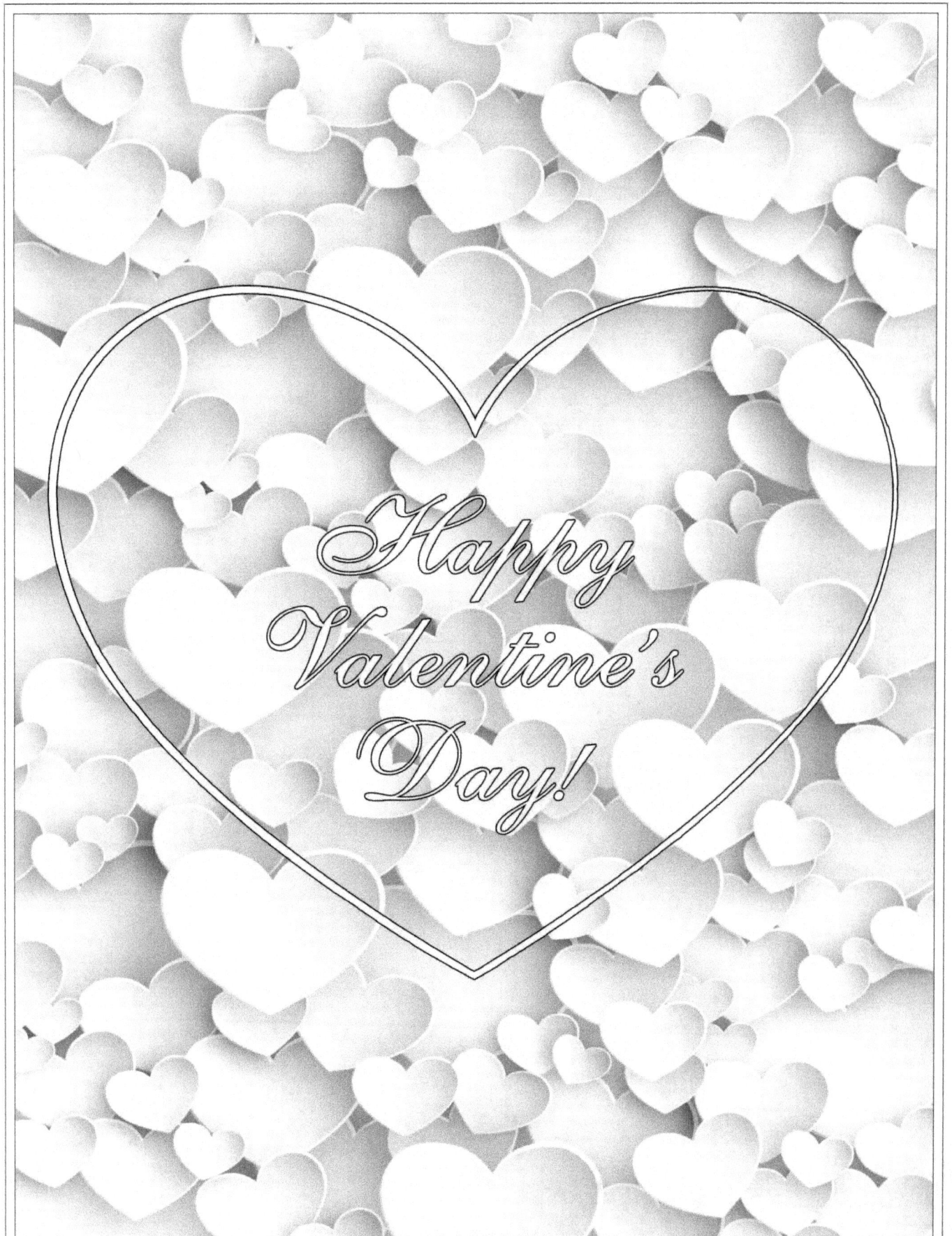

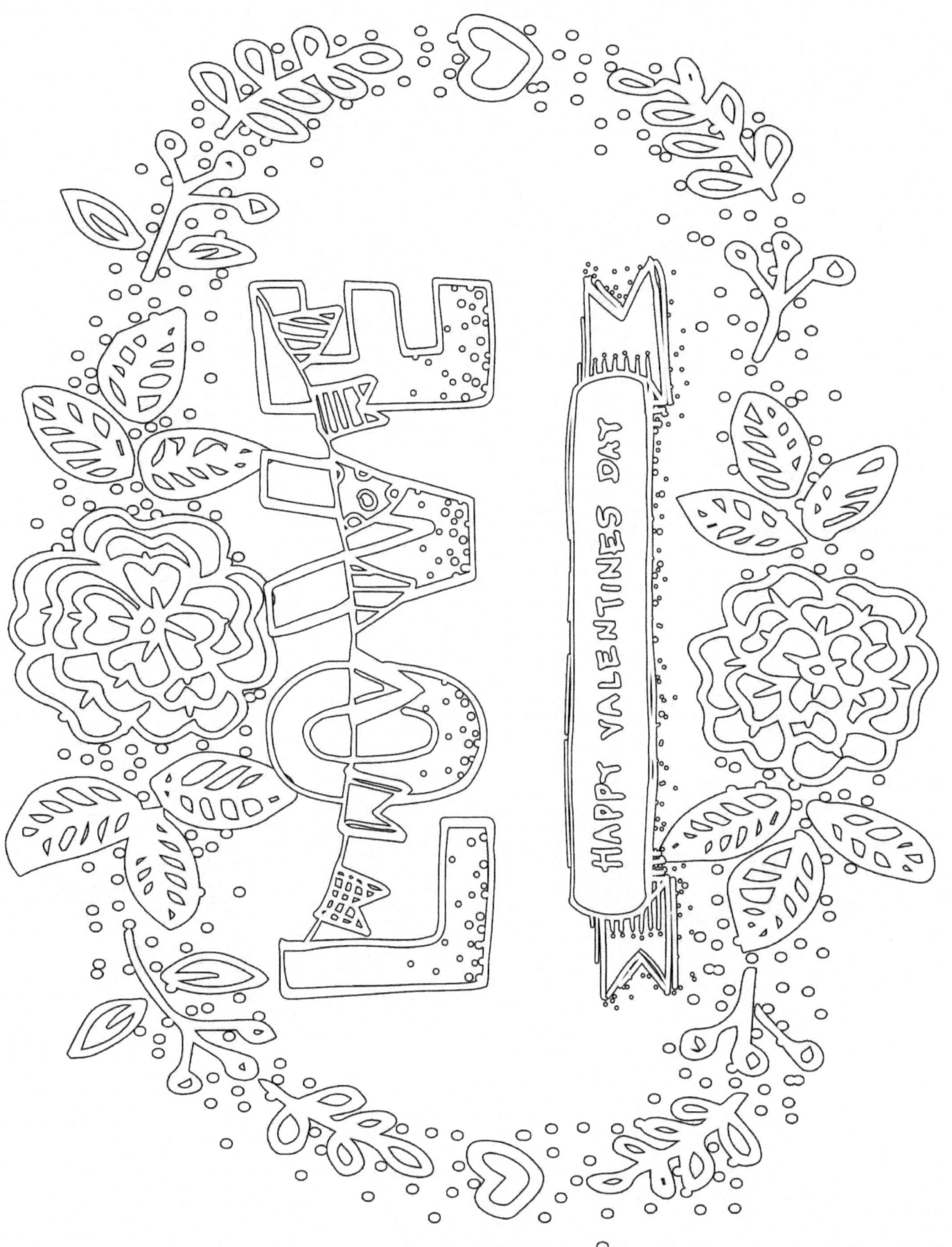

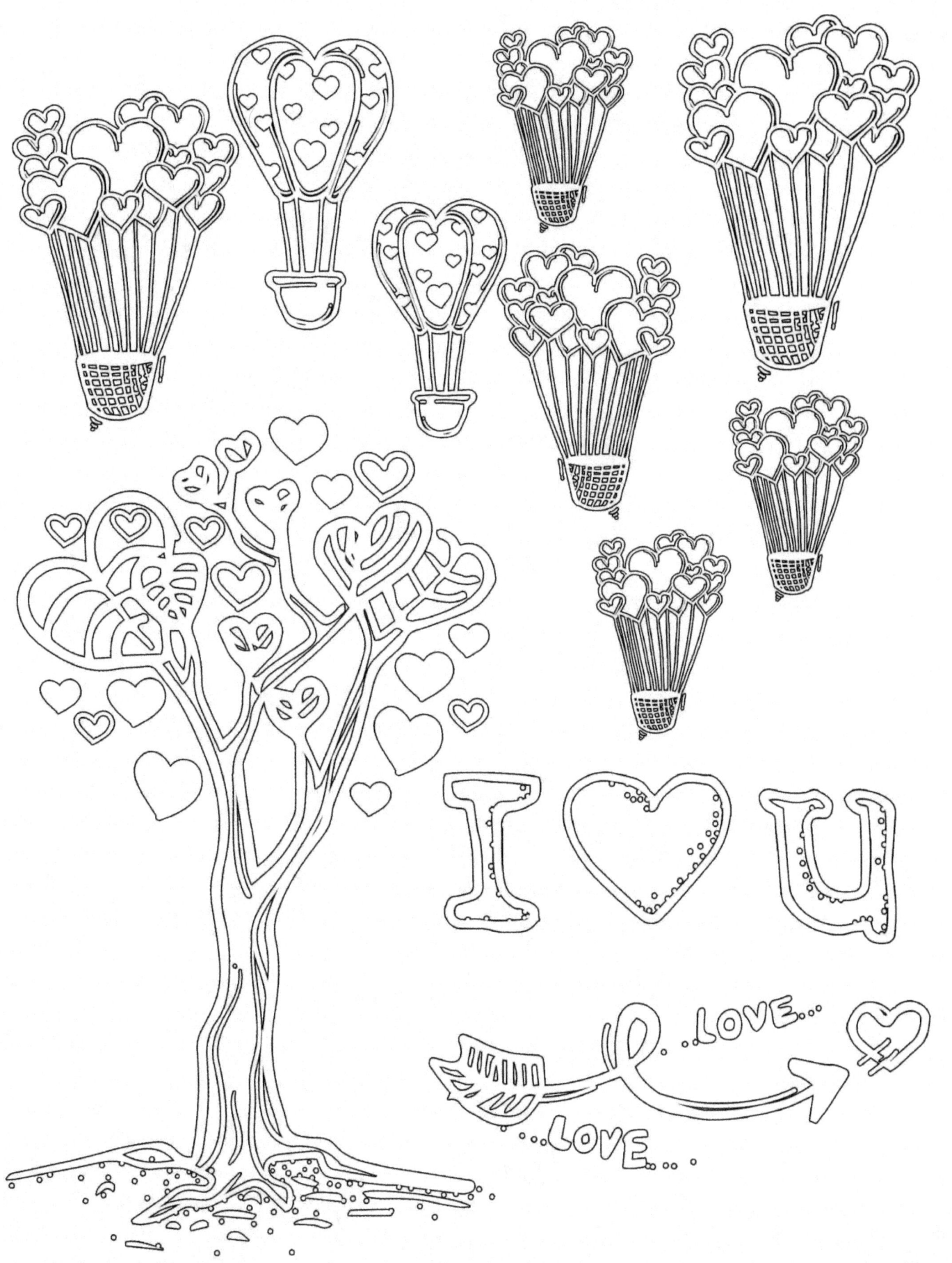

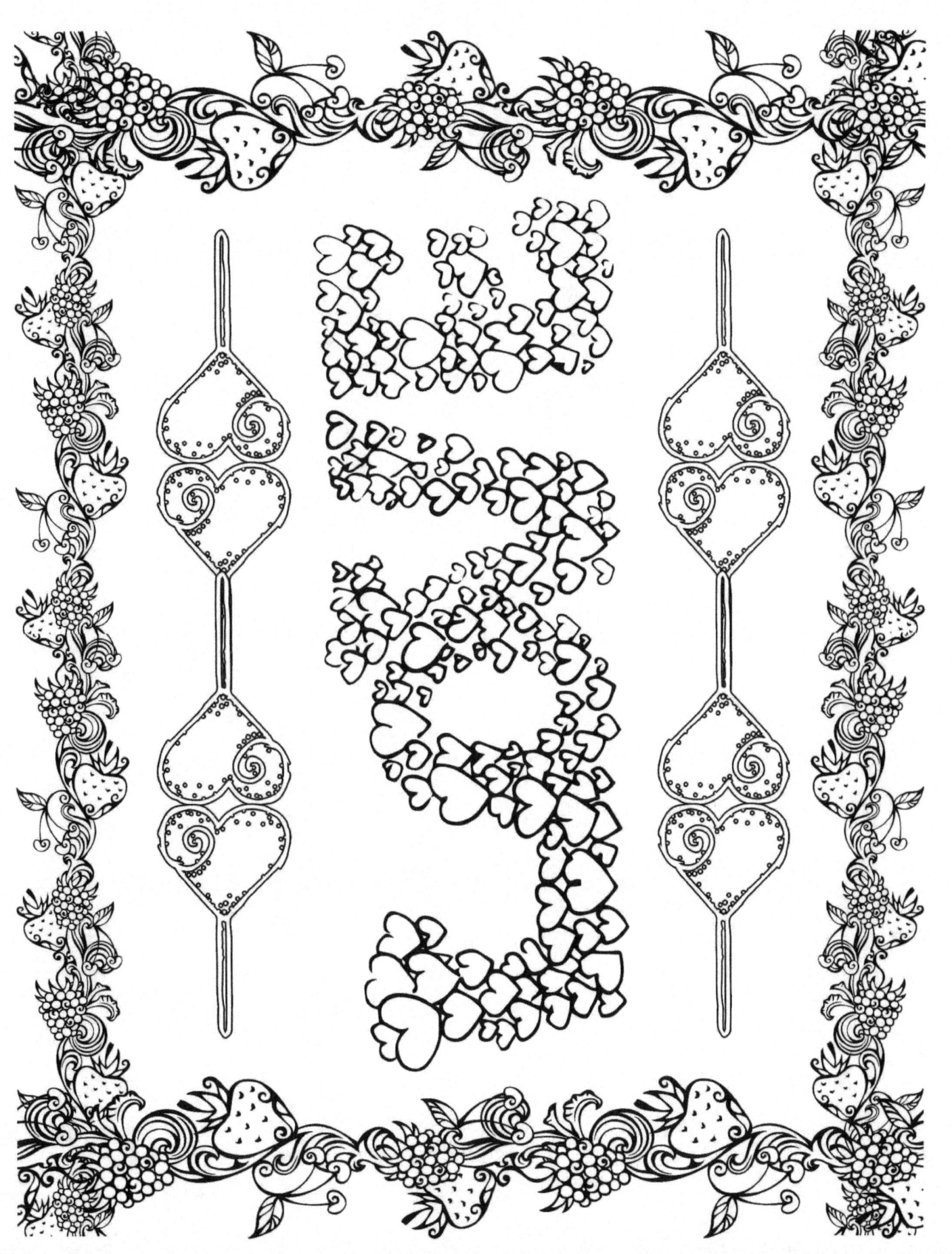

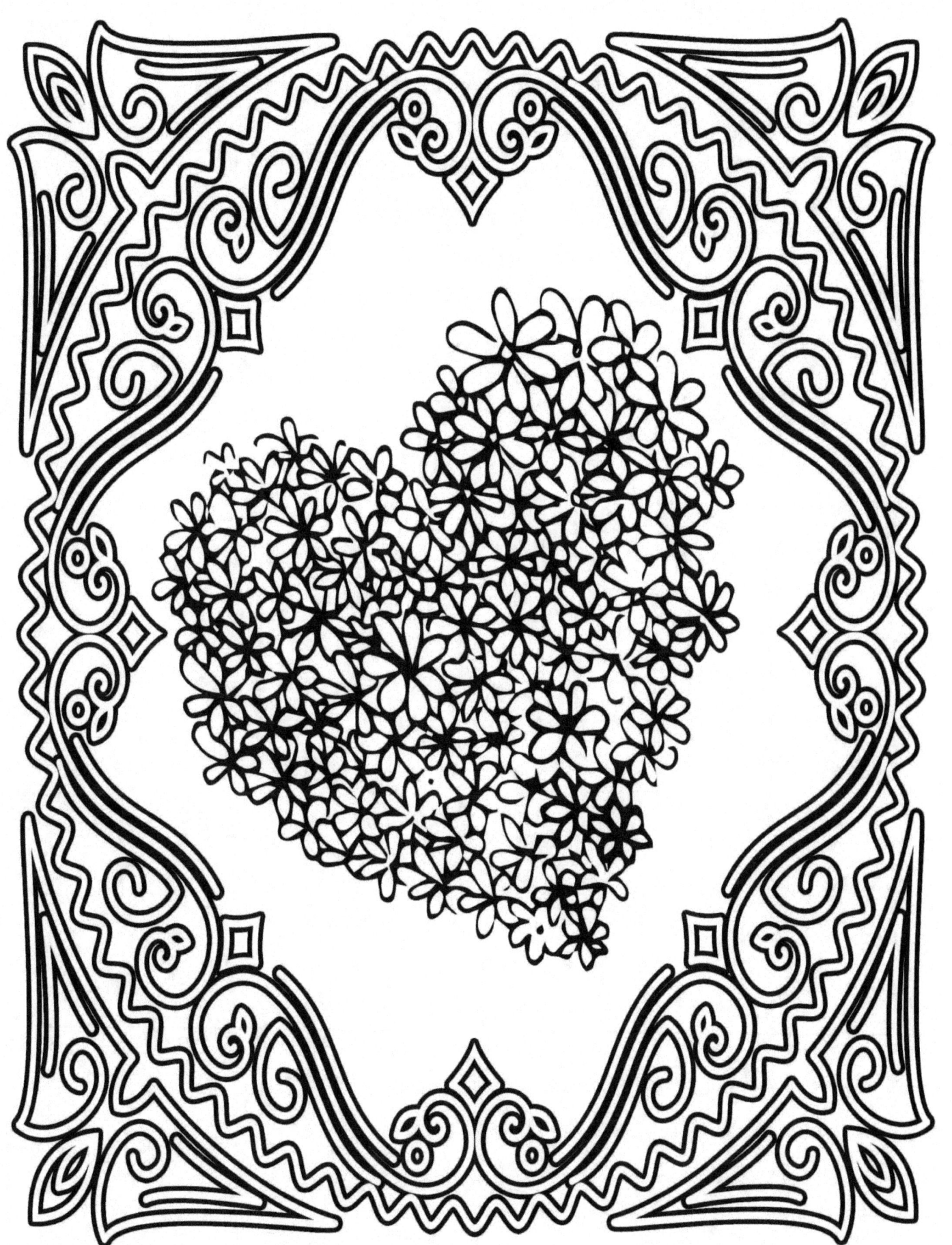

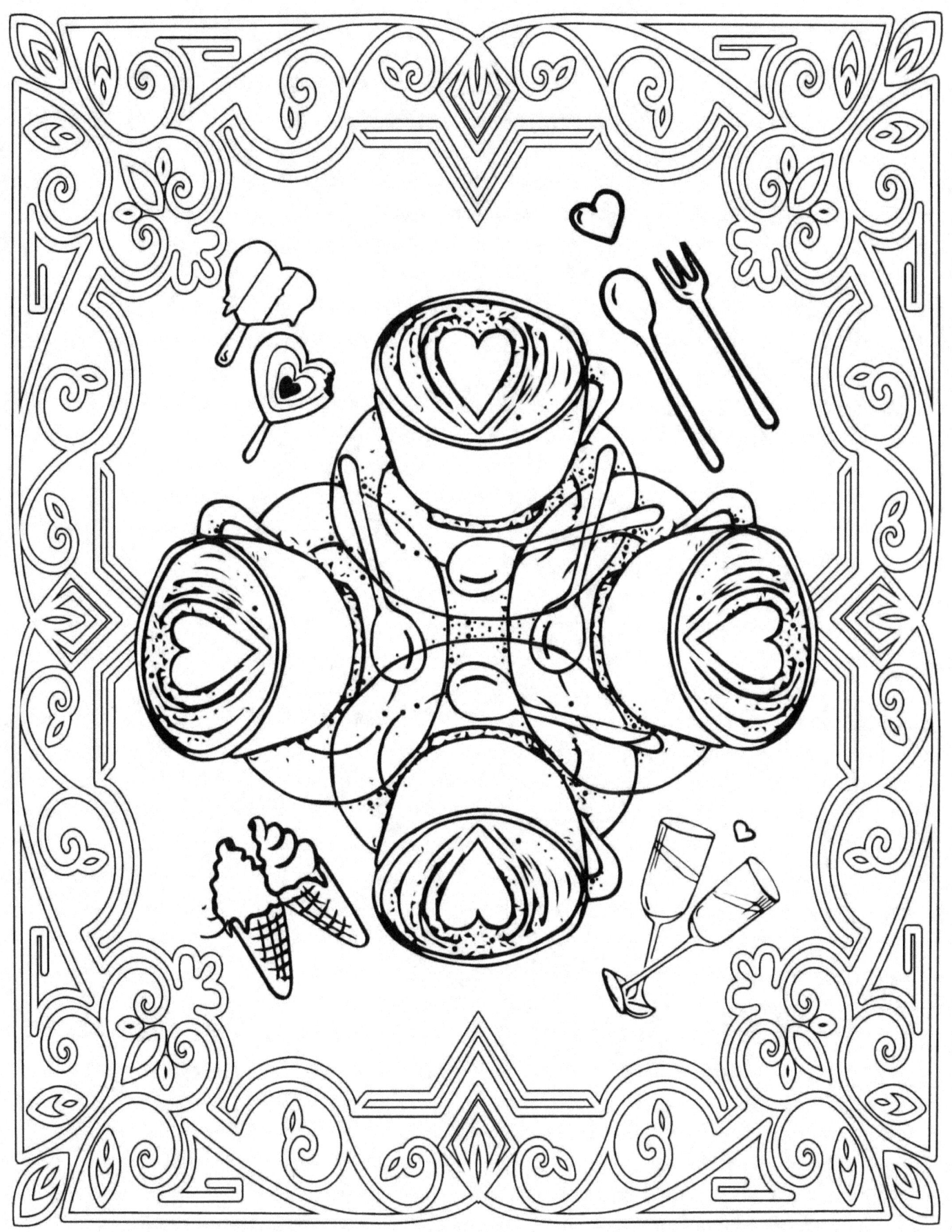

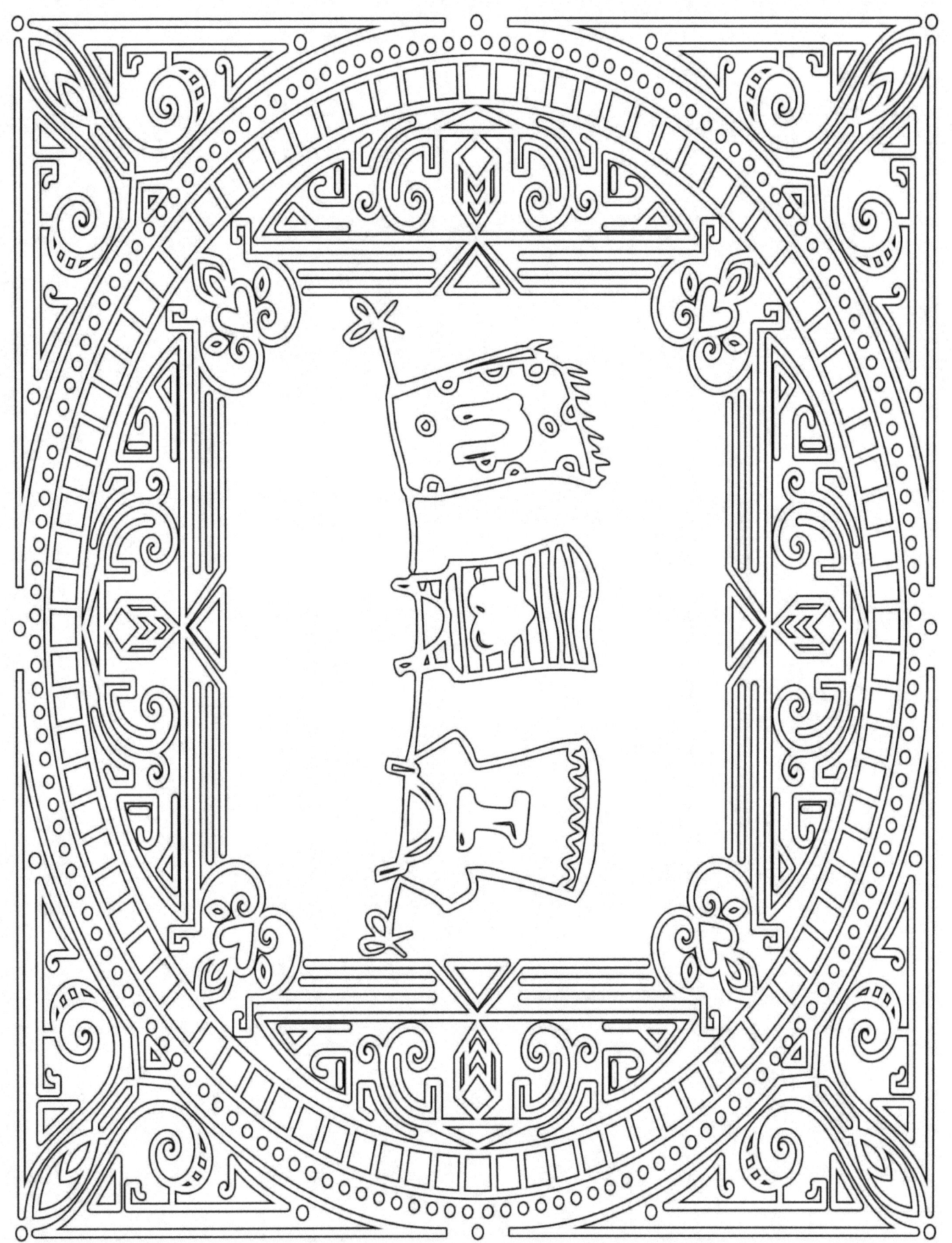

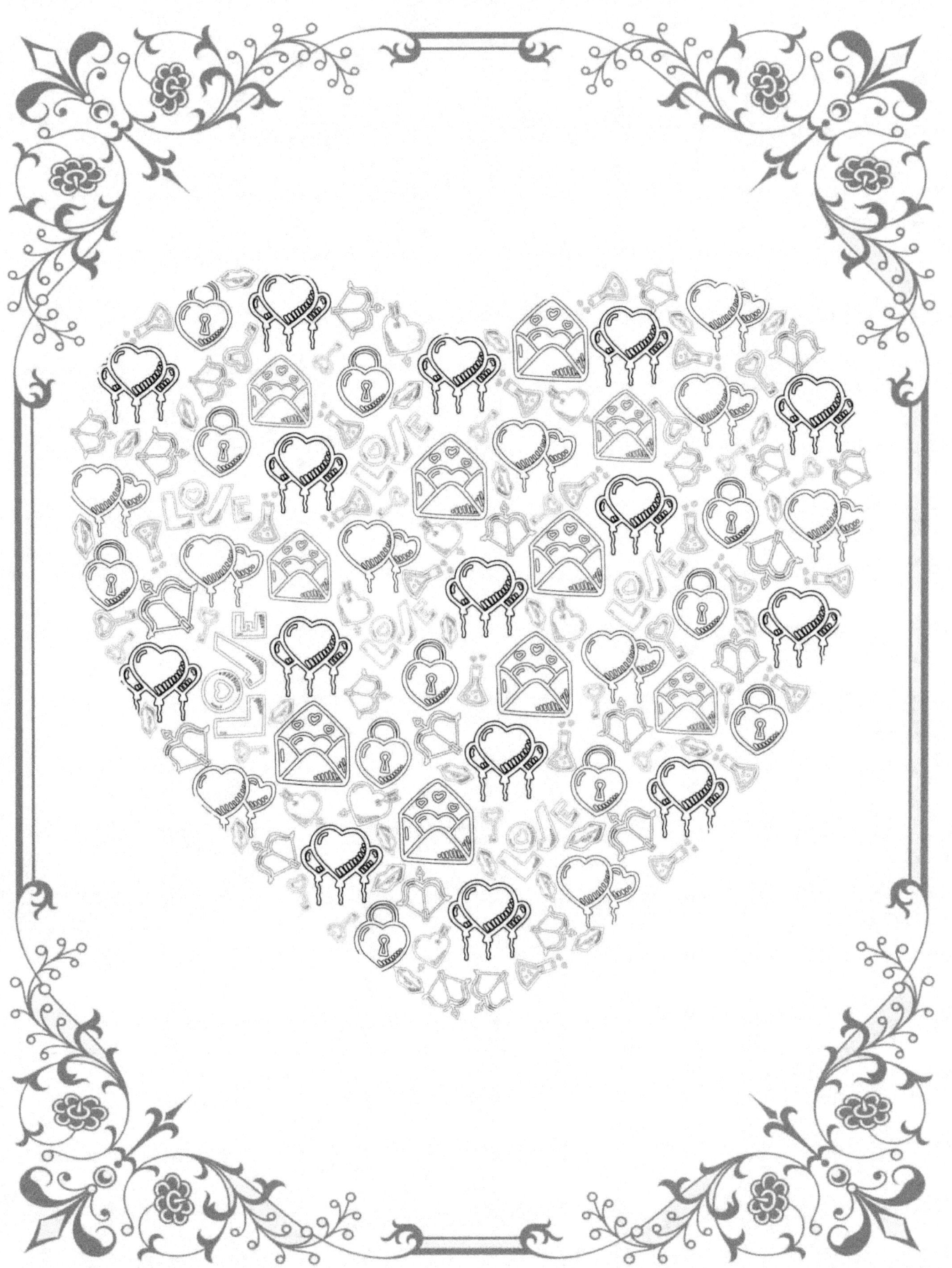

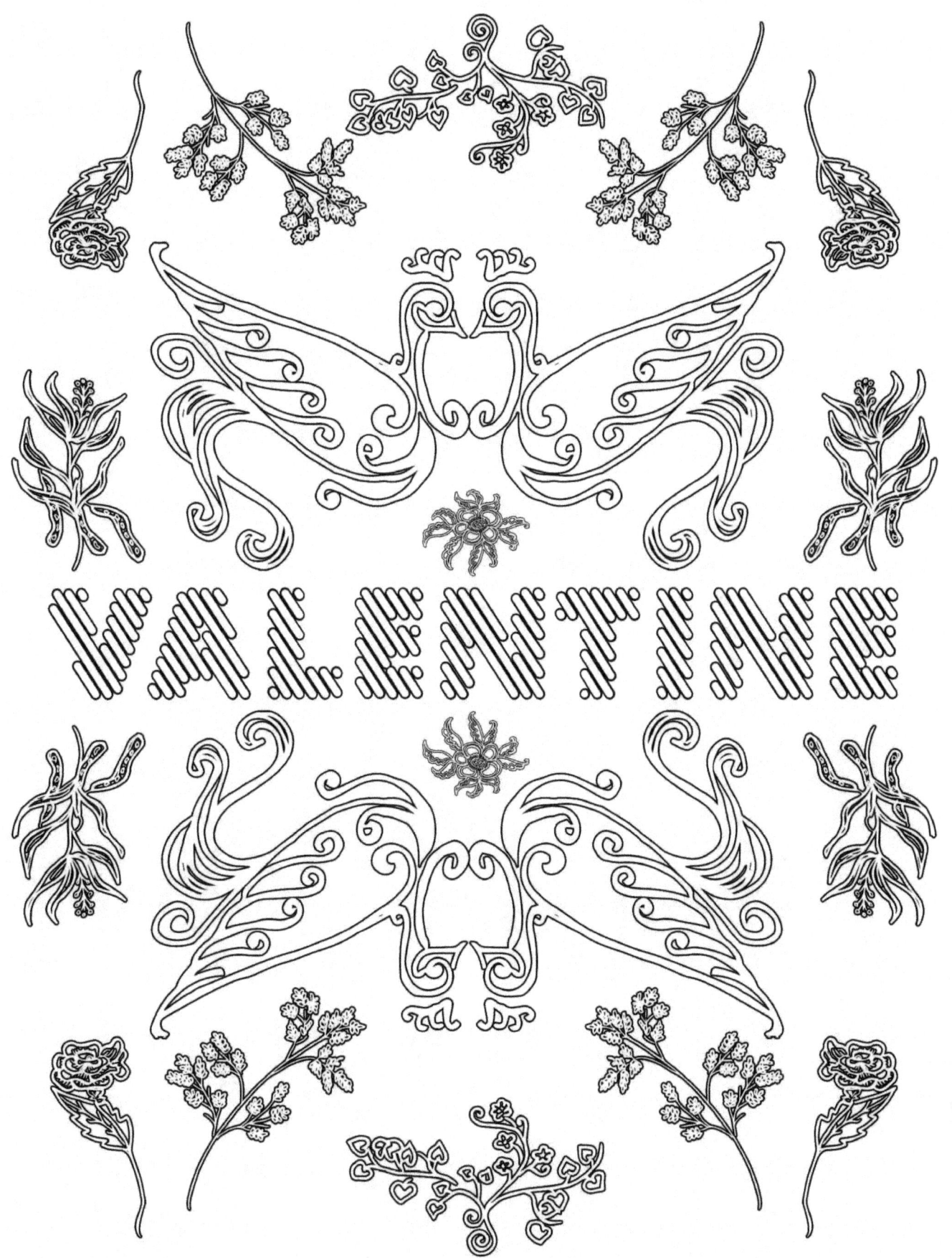

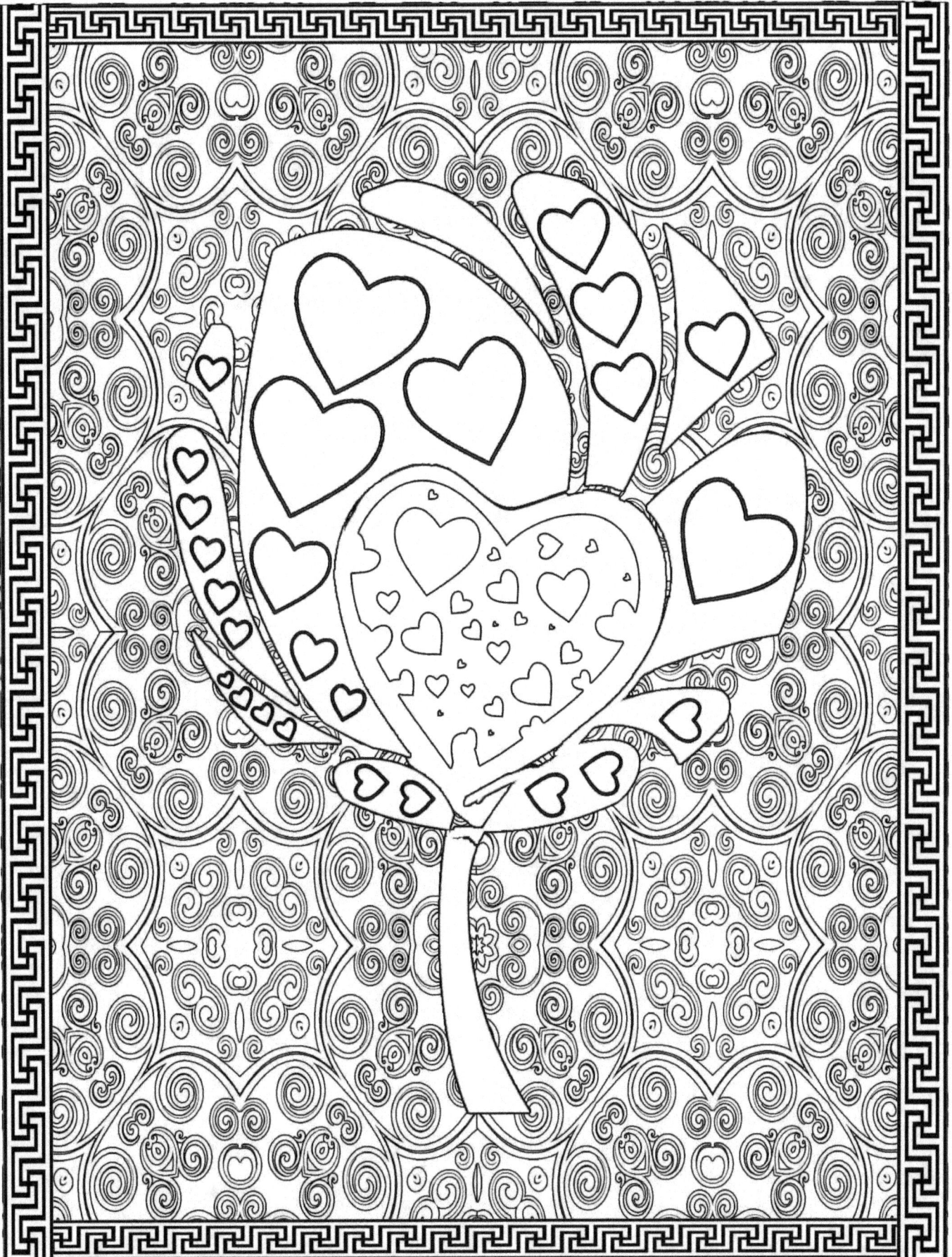

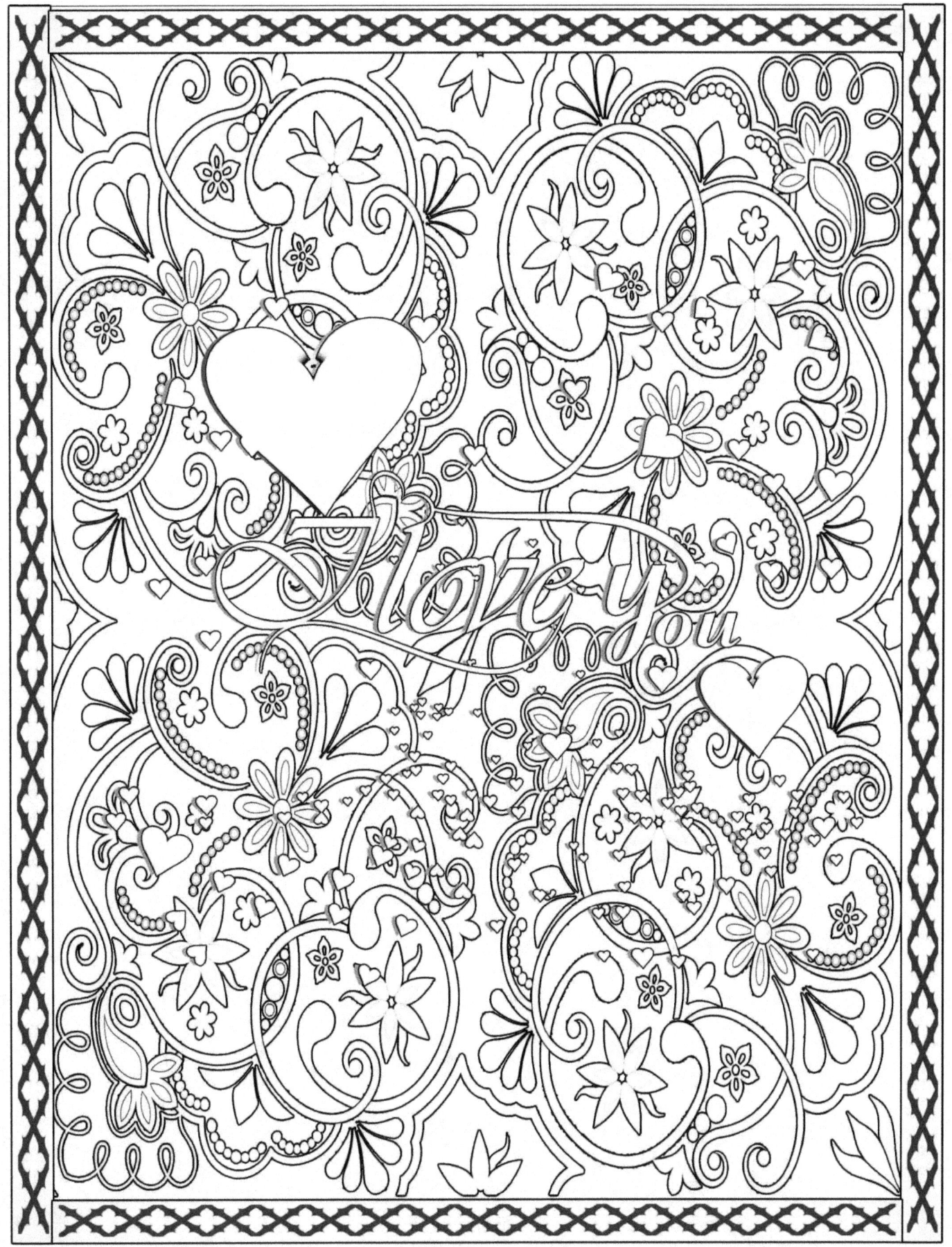

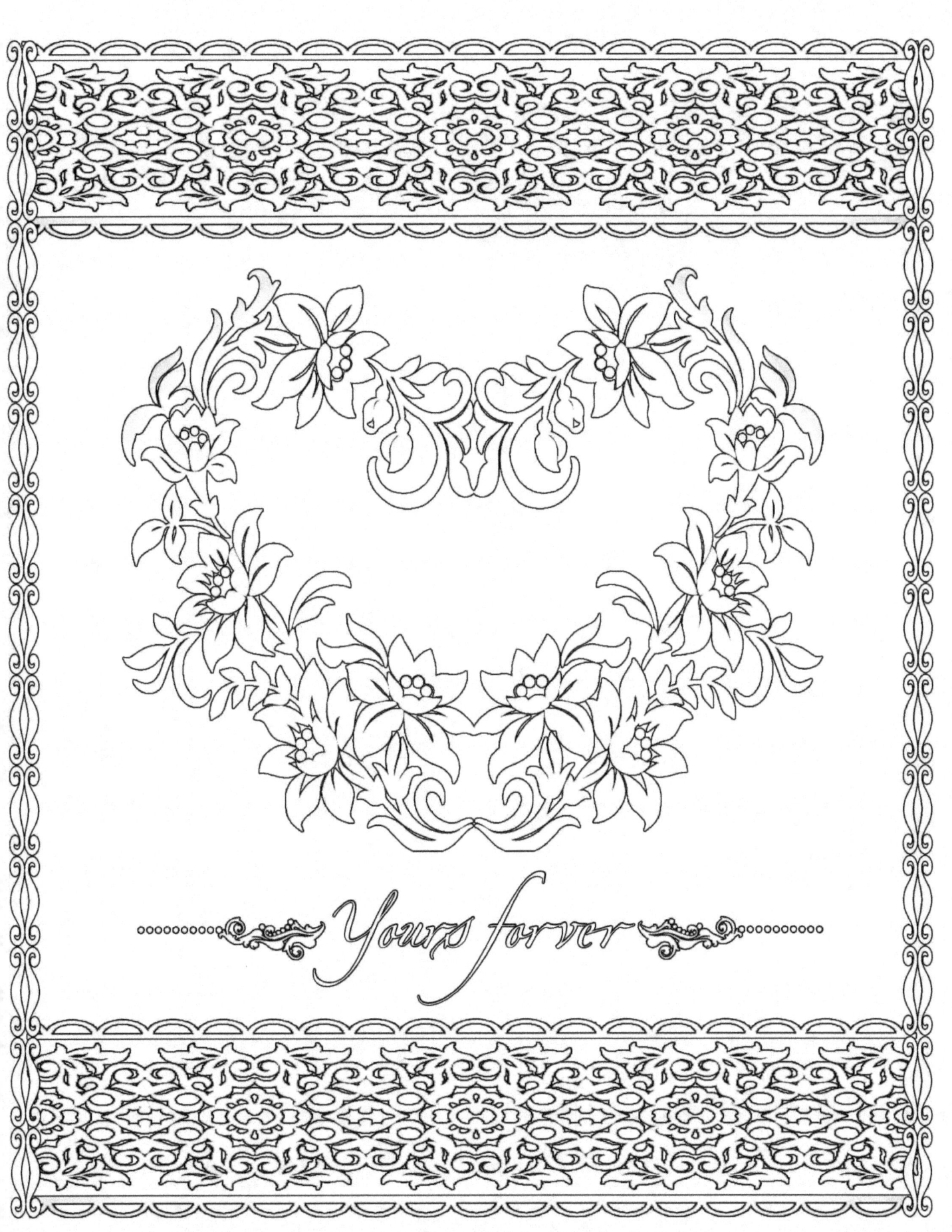

Yours forever

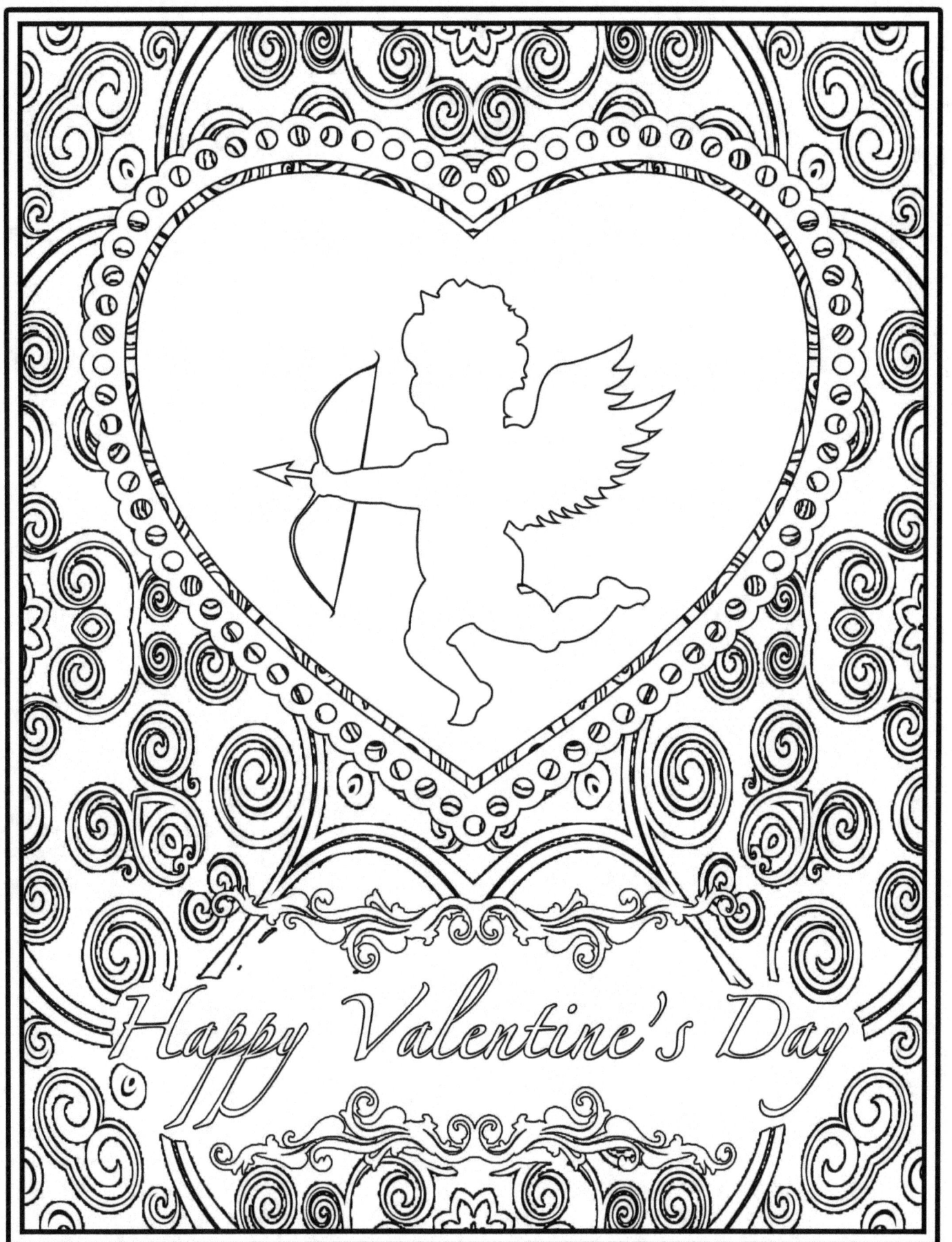

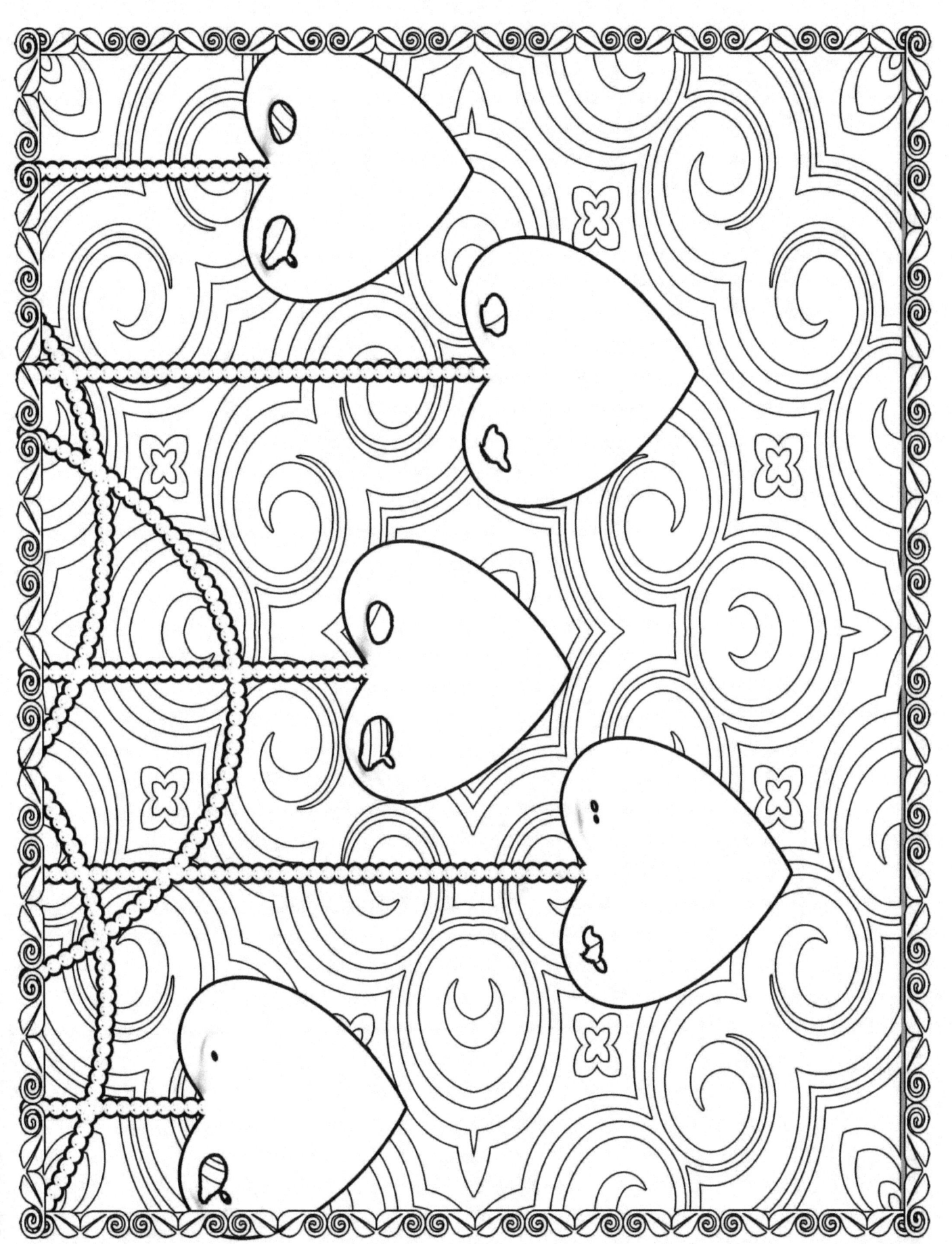

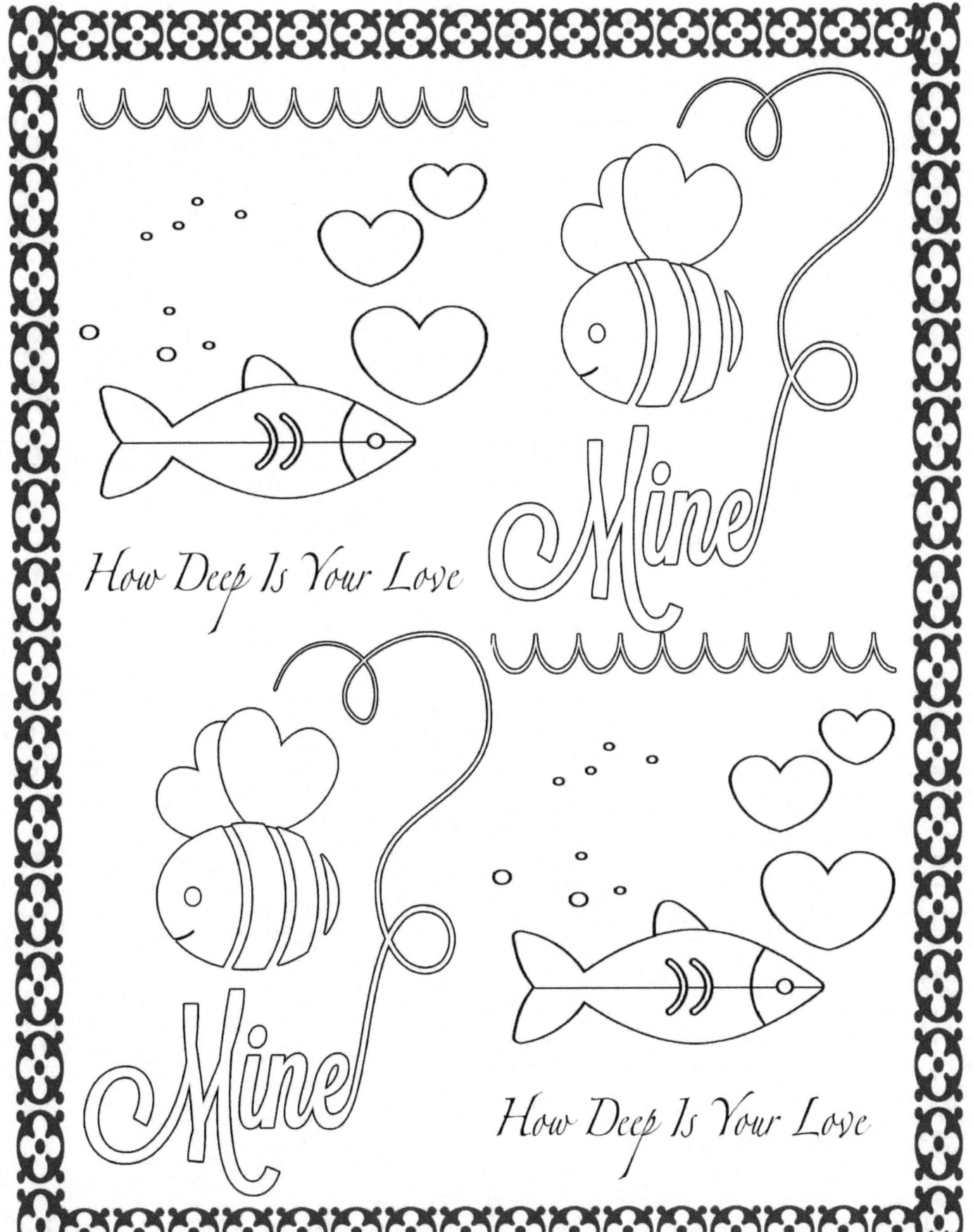

How Deep Is Your Love

Mine

Mine

How Deep Is Your Love

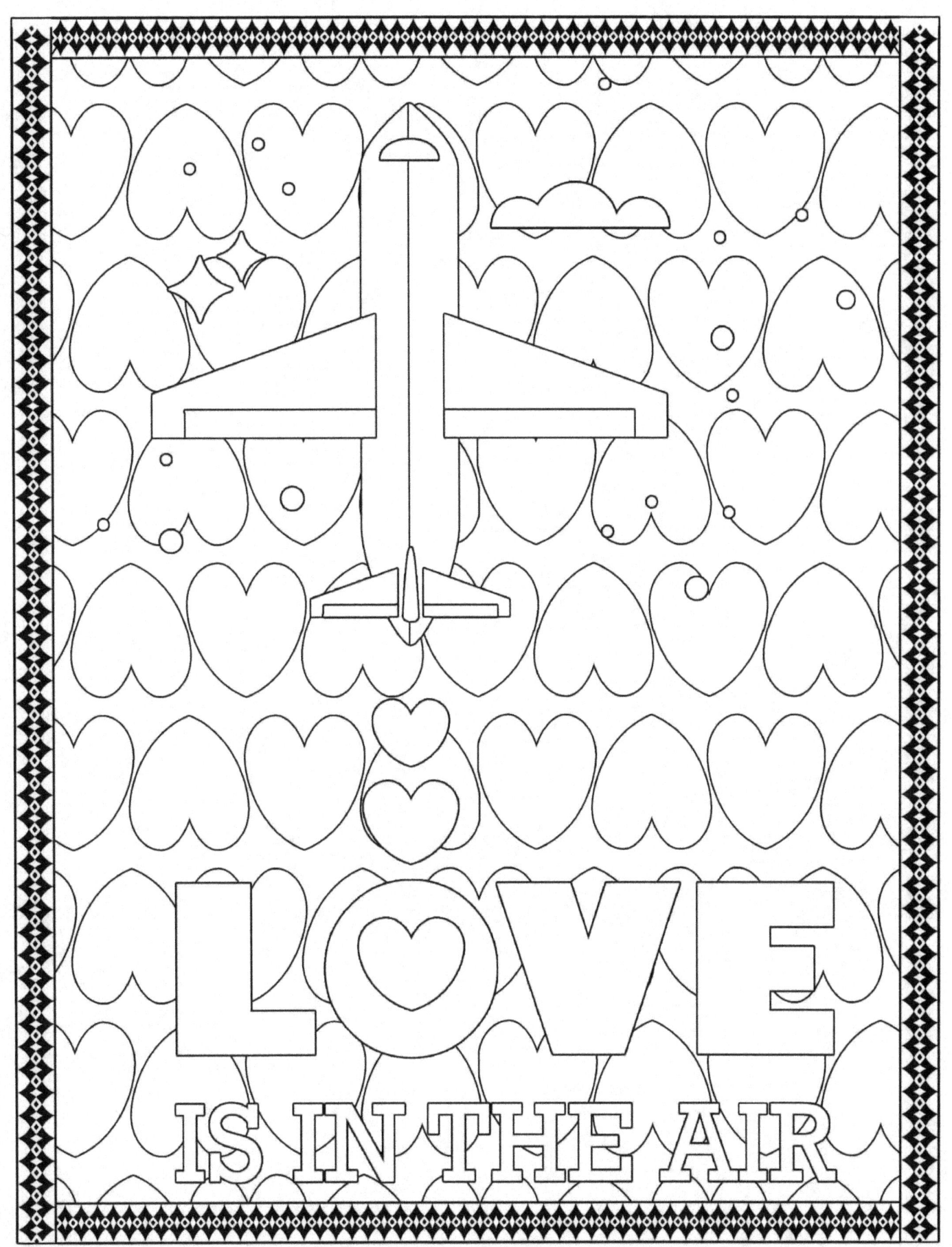

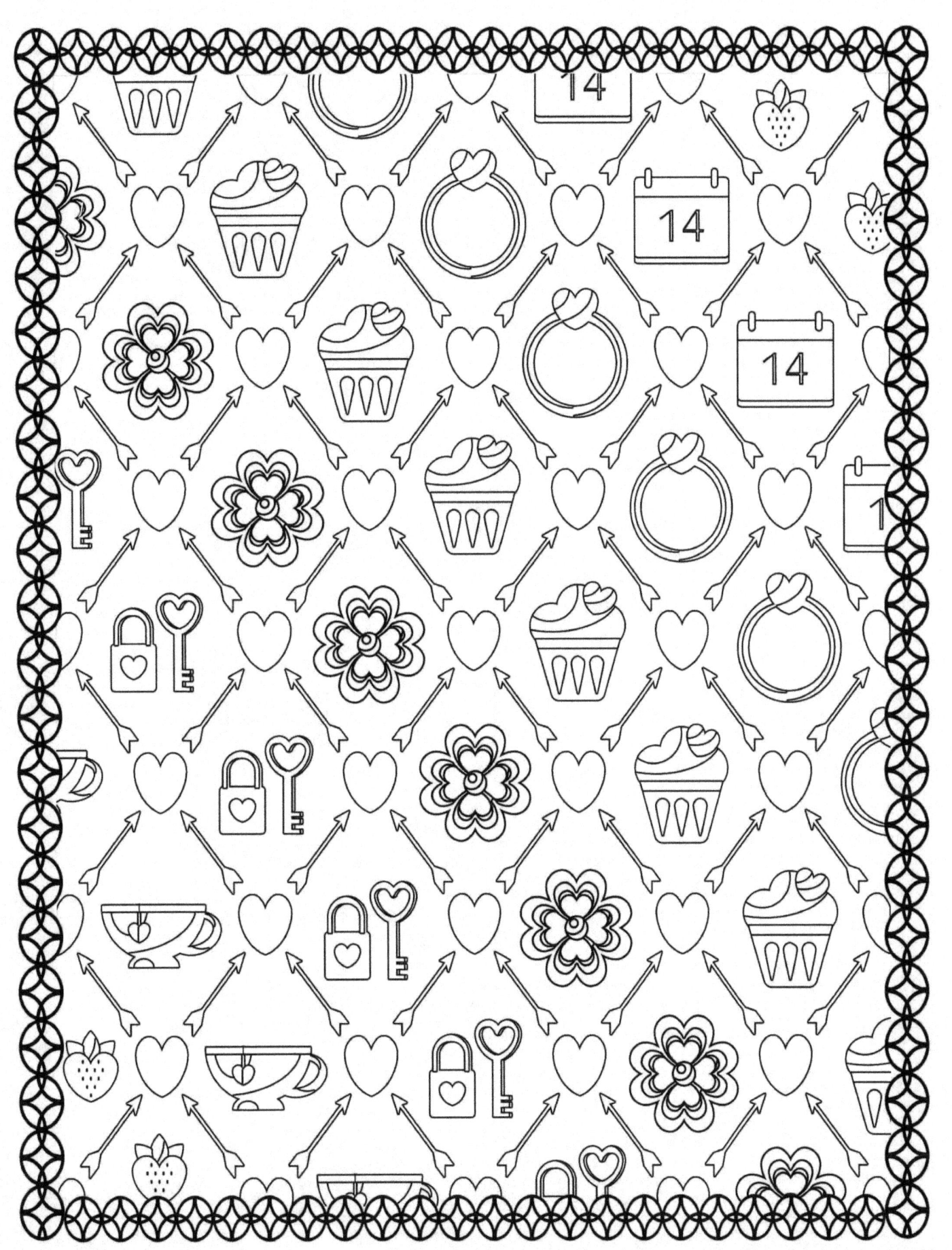

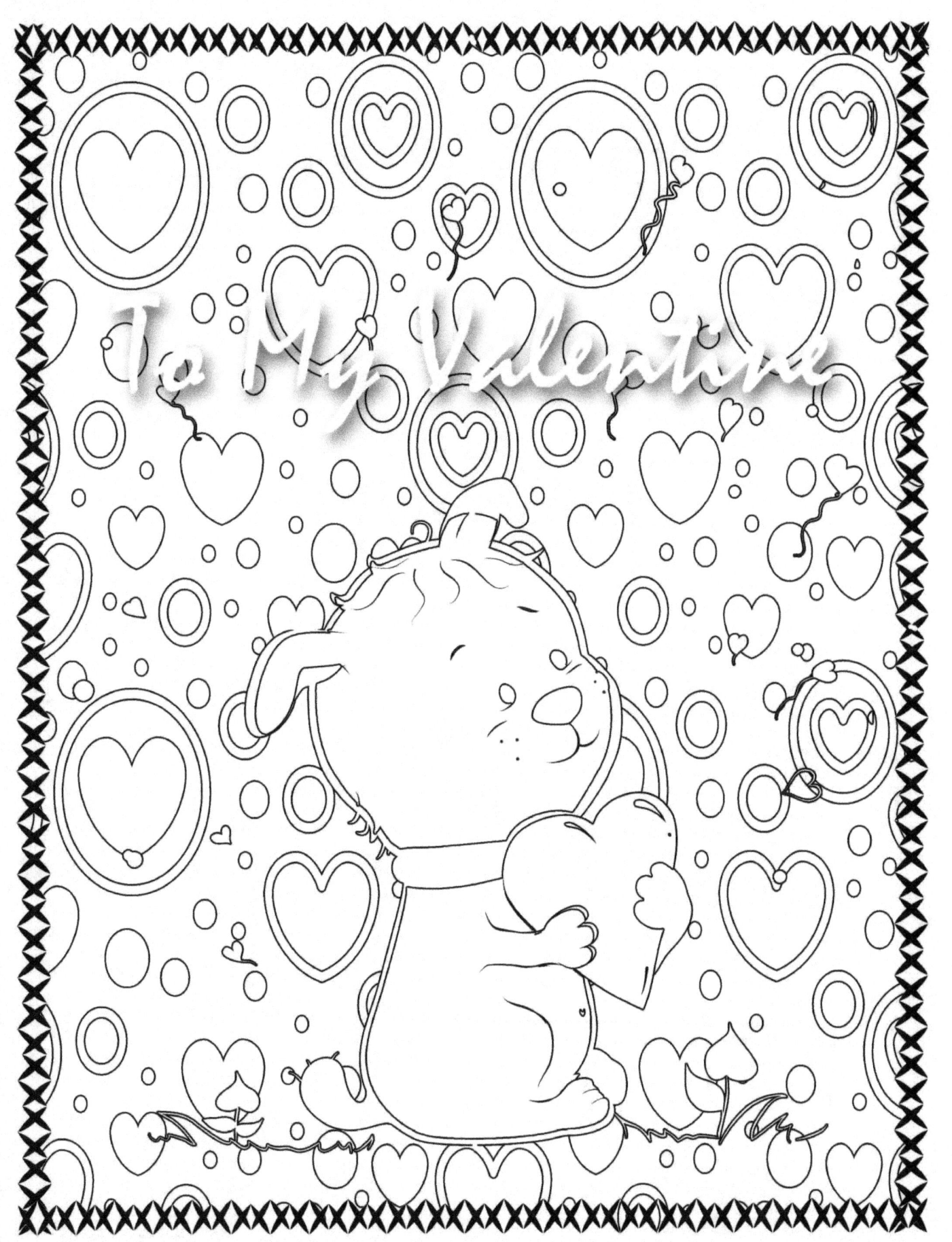

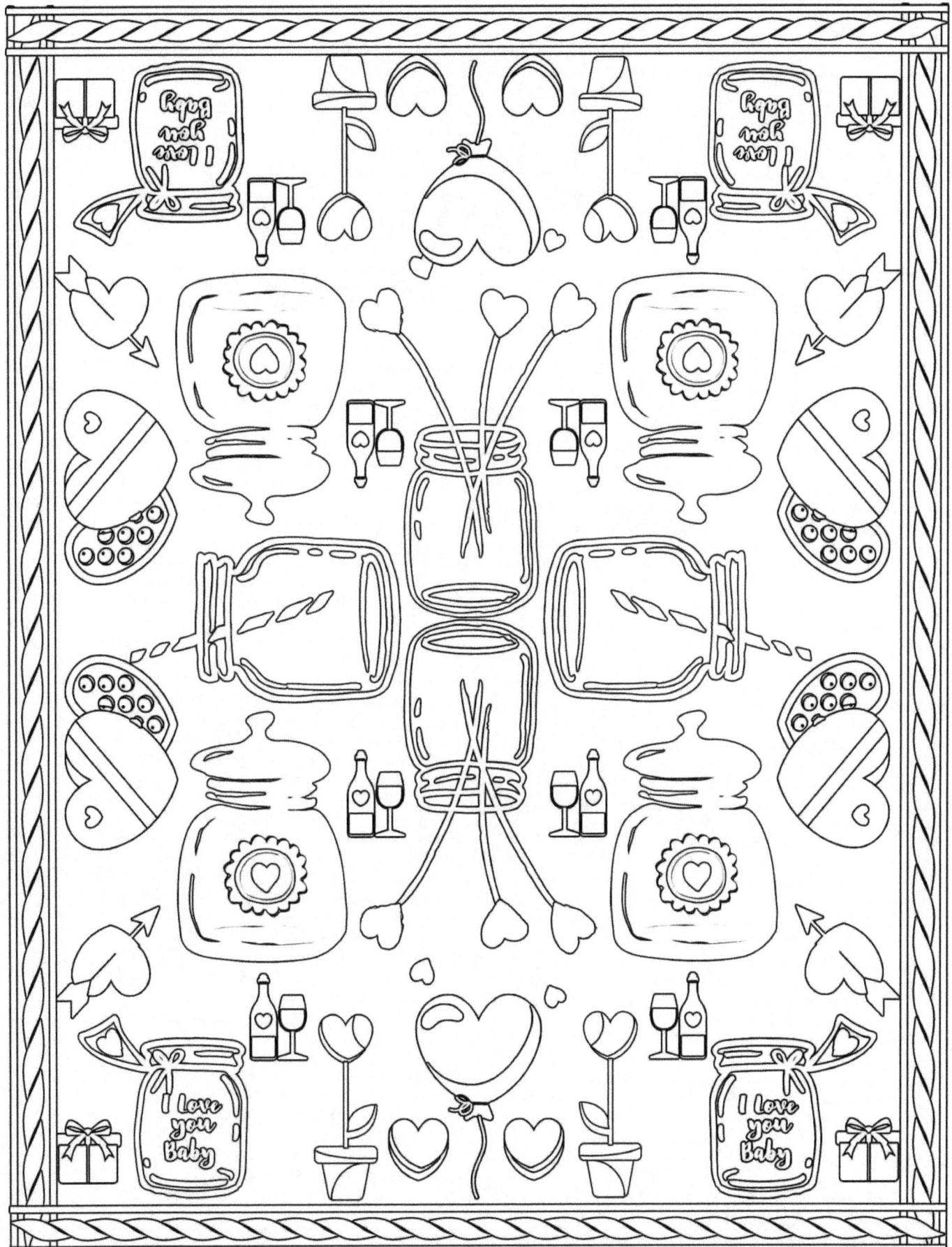

MANY THANKS FOR
PURCHASING THIS
COLOURING BOOK...

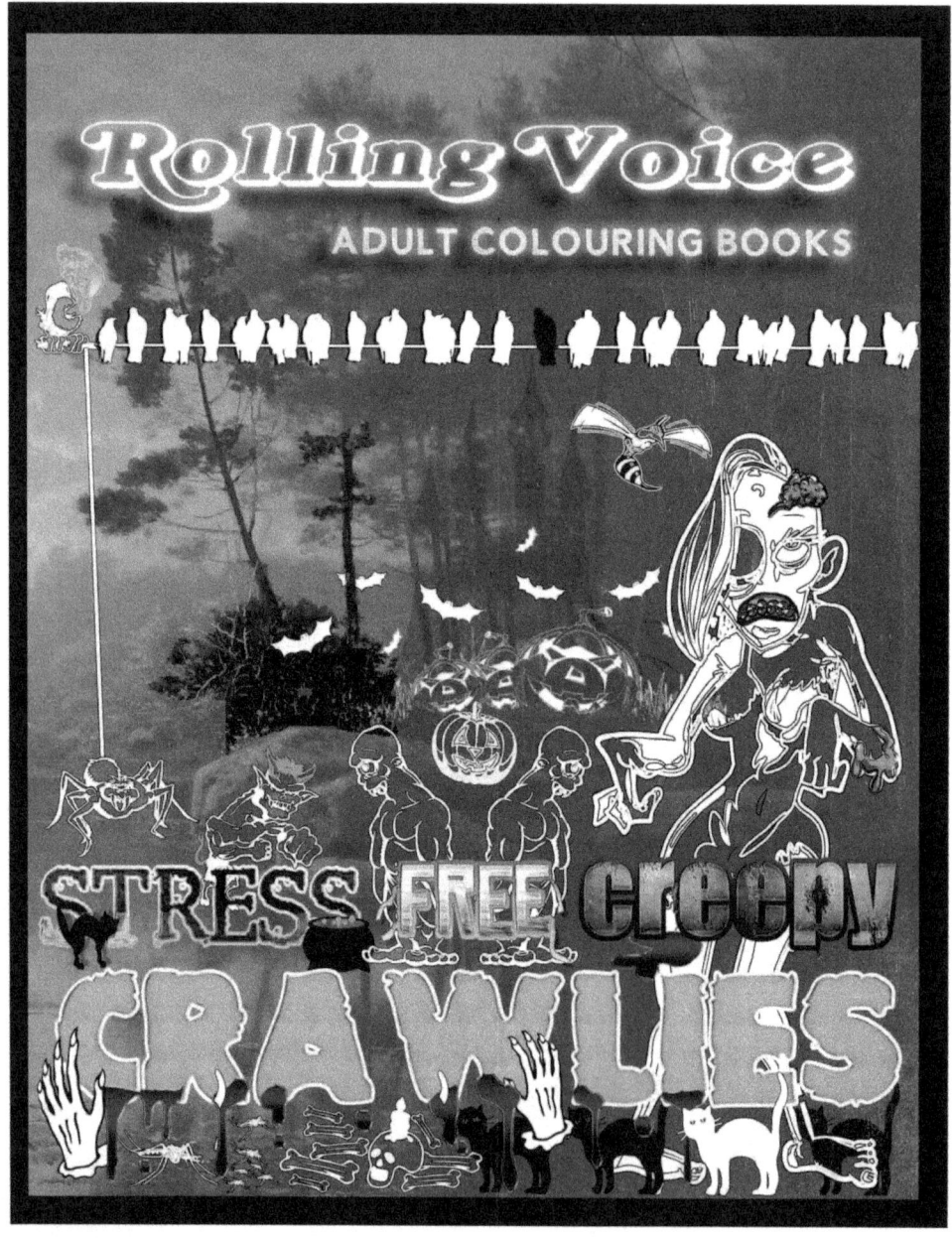

http://goo.gl/e5nKaZ
RollingVoice.com

WE HOPE YOU
HAD A JOLLY TIME
COLOURING
IT...

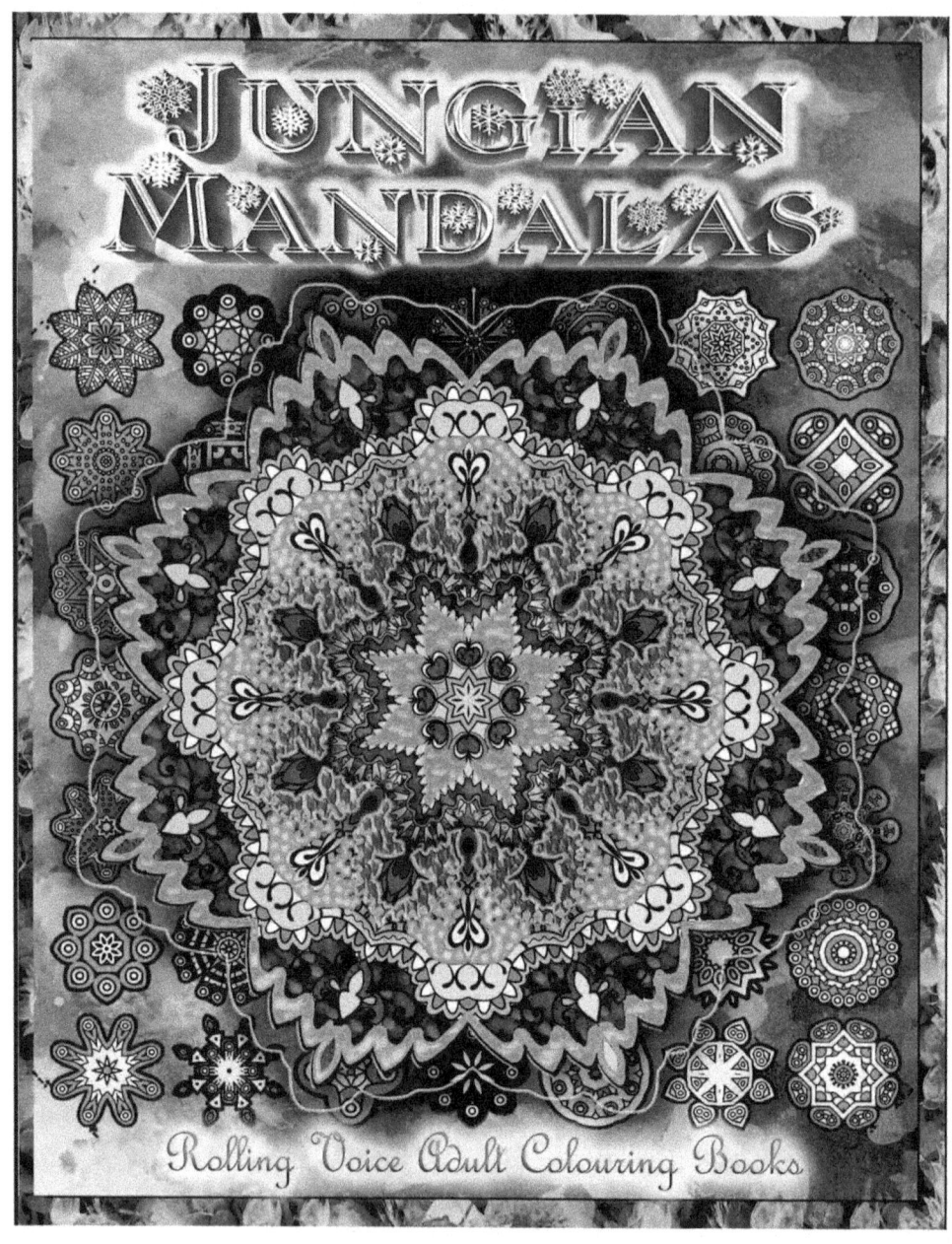

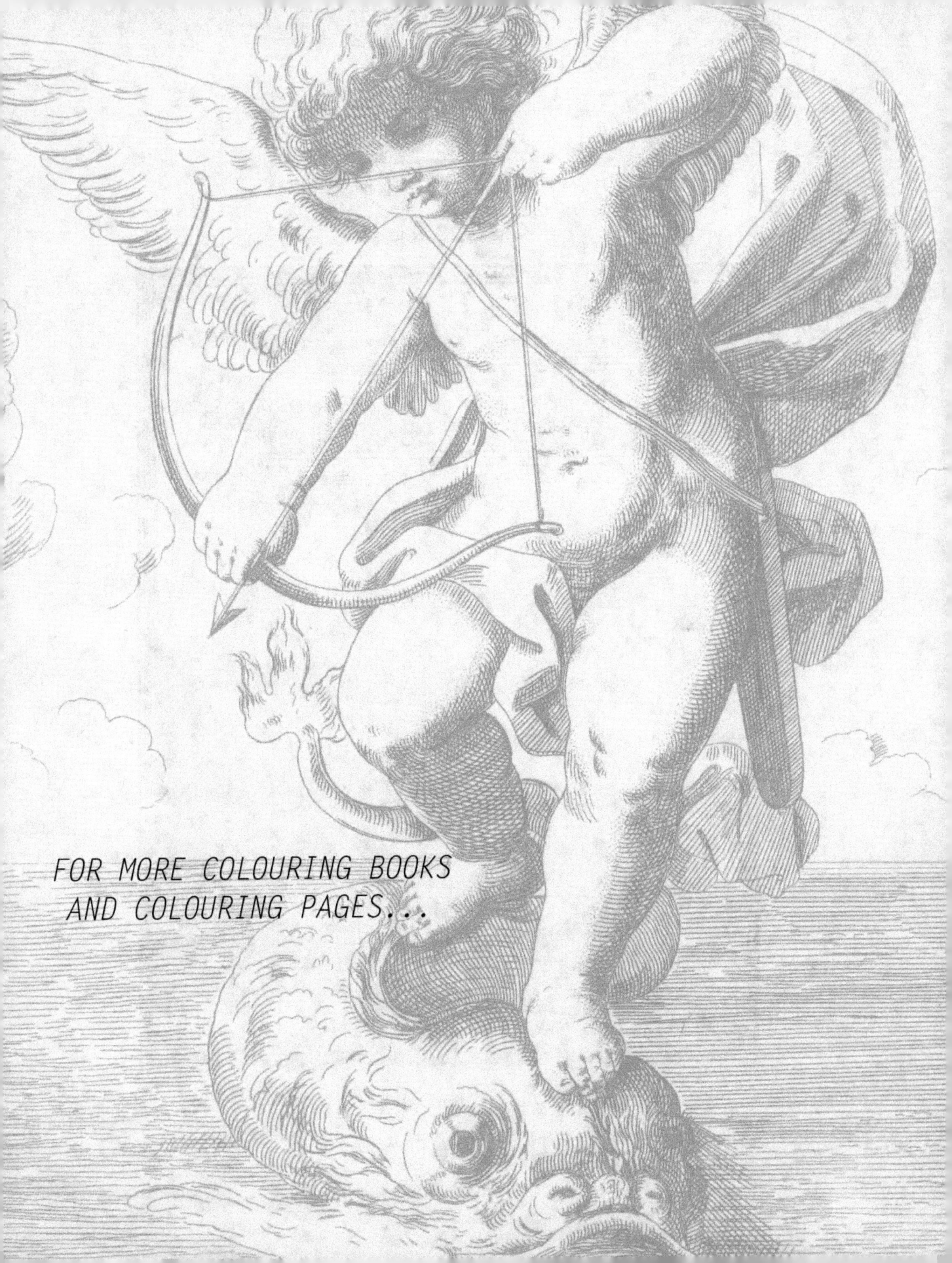

FOR MORE COLOURING BOOKS
AND COLOURING PAGES...

Other Titles by Rolling Voice

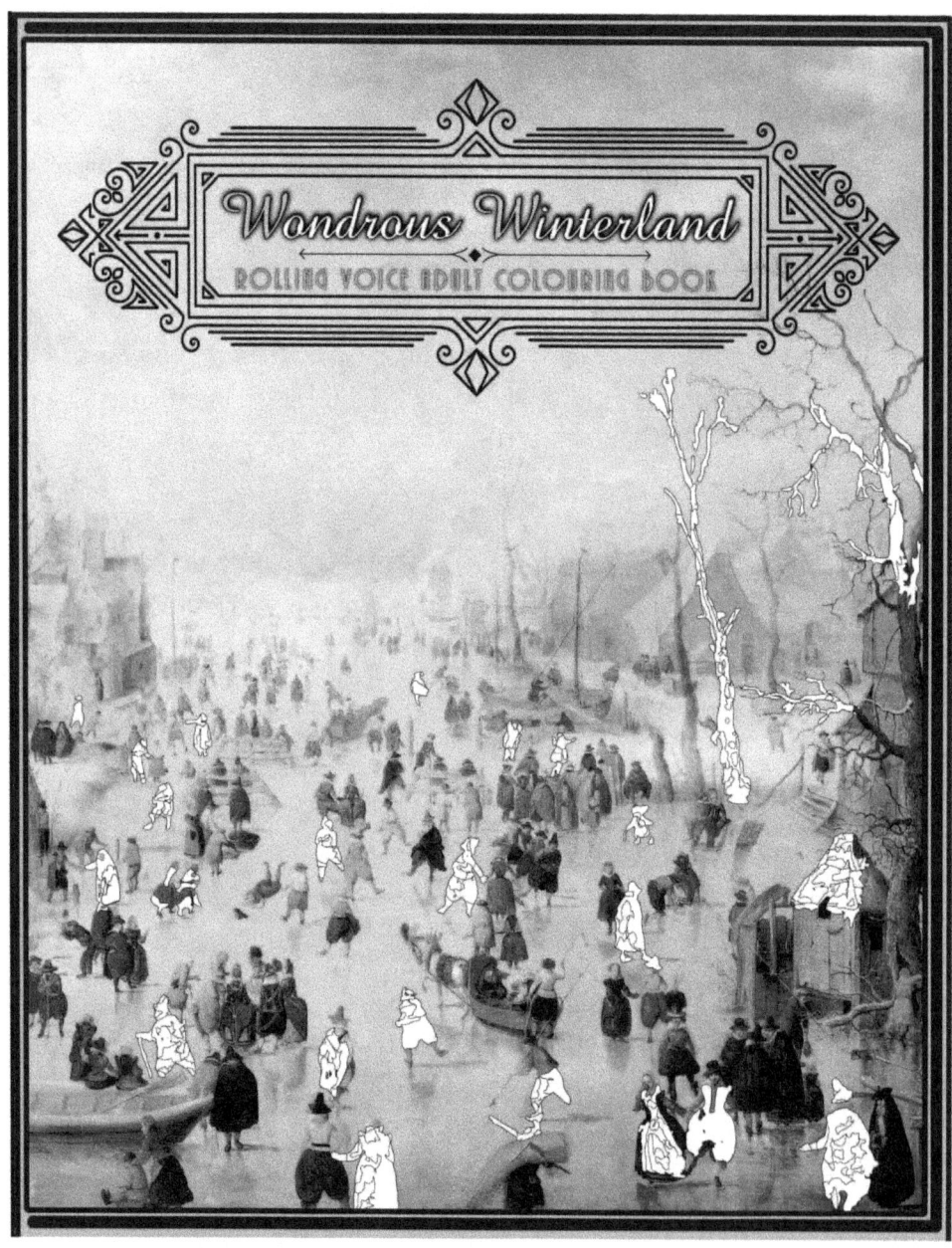

http://goo.gl/9doInv
RollingVoice.com

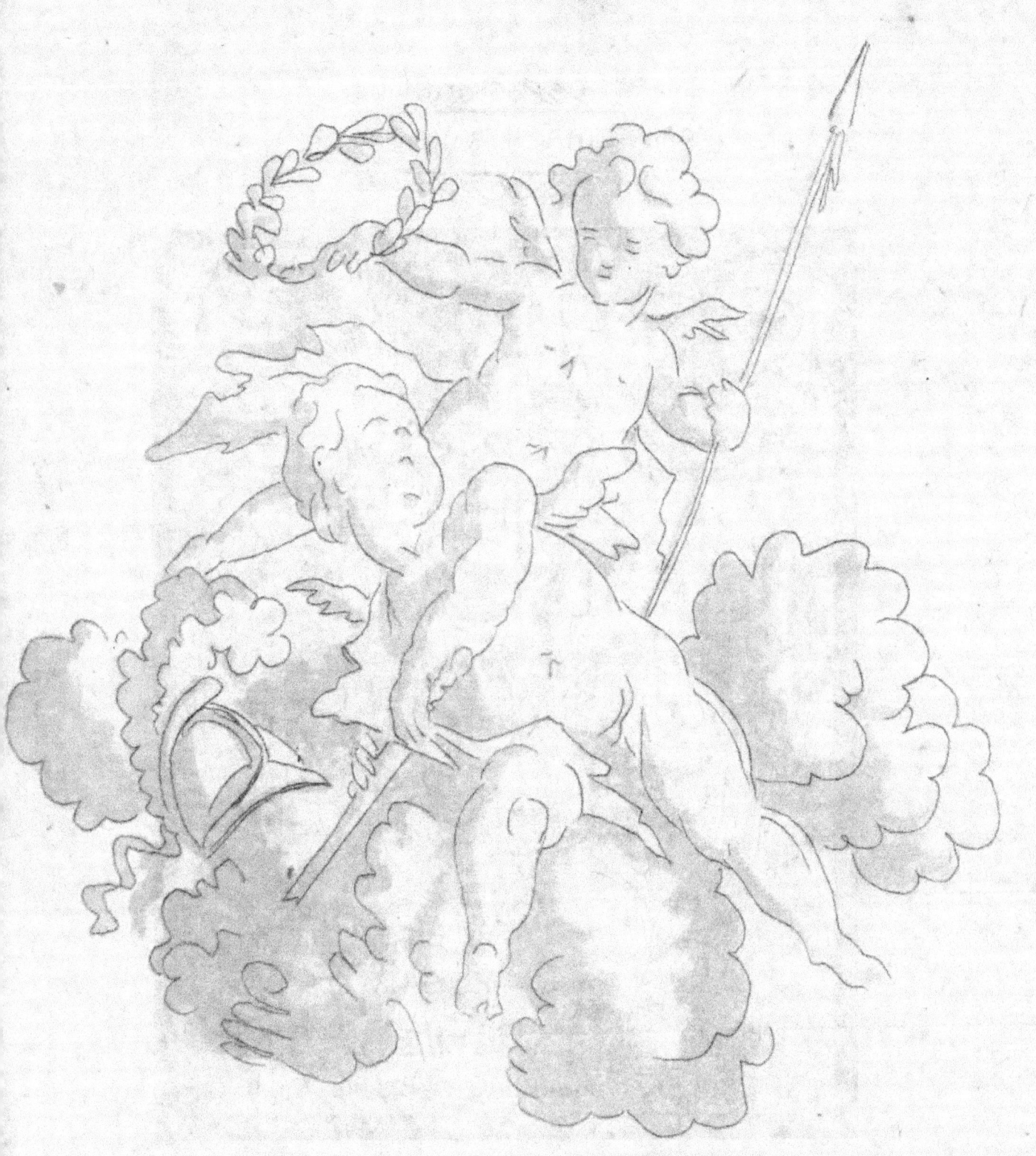

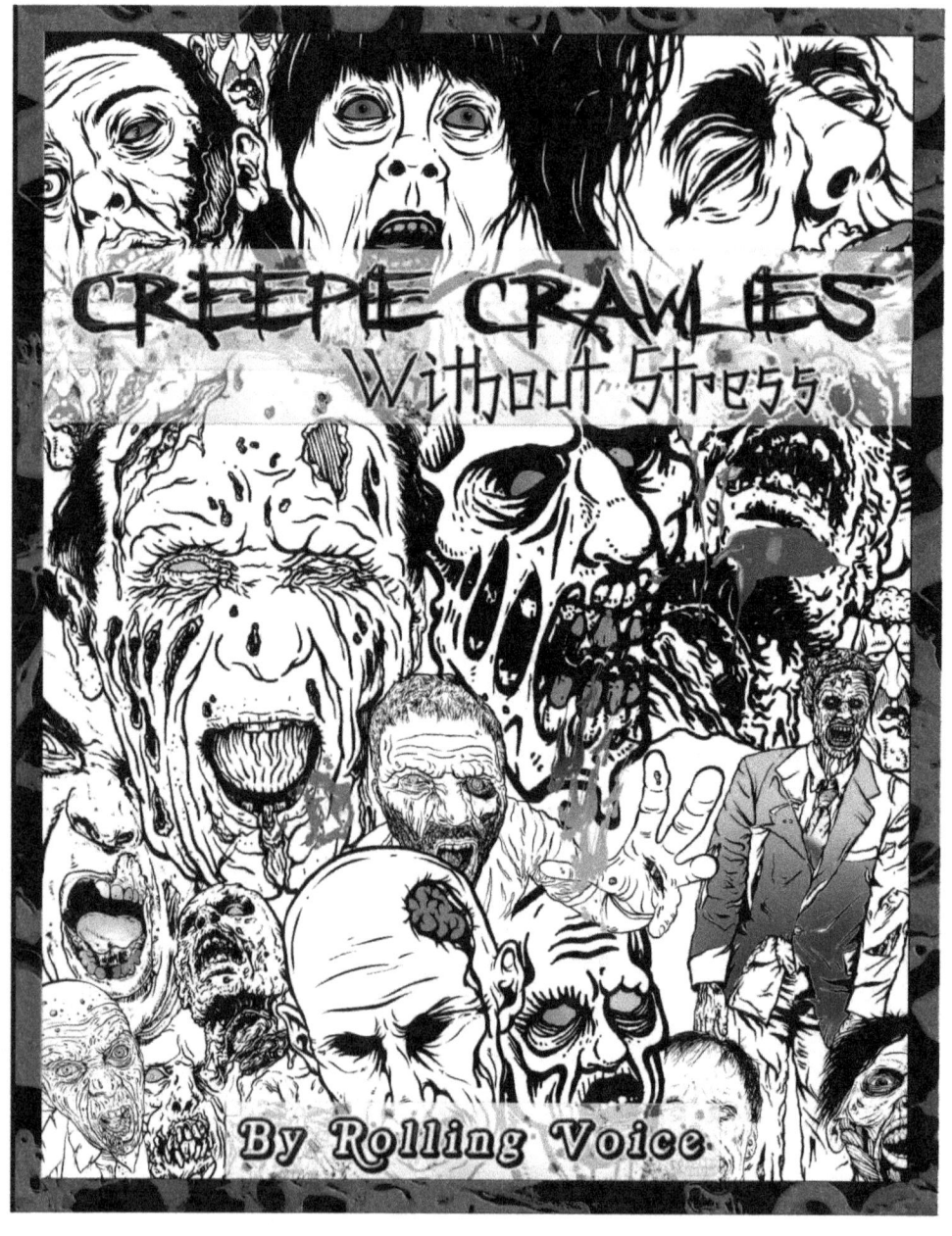

http://goo.gl/mLZJX3
RollingVoice.com

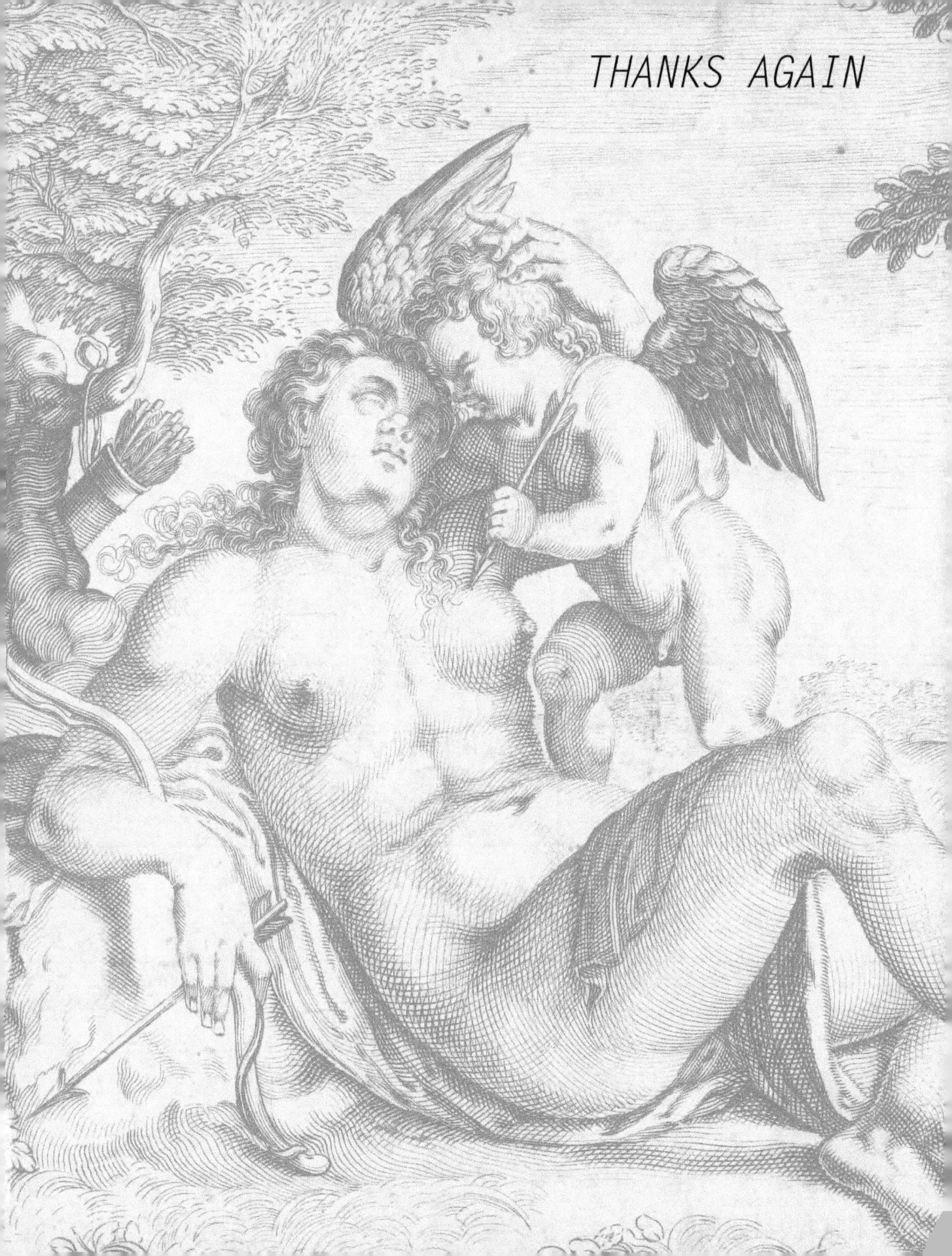

THANKS AGAIN

www.ingramcontent.com/pod-product-compliance
Lightning Source LLC
Chambersburg PA
CBHW060607210526
45169CB00028BA/2106